Learning for Success <small>Fourth Edition</small>

EFFECTIVE STRATEGIES FOR STUDENTS

Learning for Success Fourth Edition

EFFECTIVE STRATEGIES FOR STUDENTS

Joan Fleet
Fiona Goodchild
Richard Zajchowski

THOMSON

NELSON

Australia   Canada   Mexico   Singapore   Spain   United Kingdom   United States

Learning for Success: Effective Strategies for Students
Fourth Edition

by Joan Fleet, Fiona Goodchild, and Richard Zajchowski

Associate Vice President, Editorial Director:
Evelyn Veitch

Acquisitions Editor:
Mike Thompson

Marketing Manager:
Heather Leach

Senior Developmental Editor:
Rebecca Rea

Photo Researcher and Permissions Coordinator:
Terri Rothman

Production Editor:
Julie van Veen

Copy Editor/Proofreader:
Kelli Howey

Indexer:
Jin Tan

Production Coordinator:
Ferial Suleman

Design Director:
Ken Phipps

Interior Design:
Katherine Strain

Cover Design:
Rachel Sloat

Cover Image:
© Veer

Compositor:
Carol Magee

Printer:
Webcom

Library and Archives Canada Cataloguing in Publication

Fleet, Joan, 1939–
  Learning for success : effective strategies for students / Joan Fleet, Fiona Goodchild, Richard Zajchowski. — 4th ed.

Includes index.
ISBN 0-17-641529-7

  1. Study skills. I. Goodchild, Fiona, 1943– II. Zajchowski, Richard III. Title.

LB1049.F48 2005   378.1'7'0281
C2005-900975-6

CONTENTS

Preface   ix

Acknowledgments   xiv

Part 1
HOW TO BE A STRATEGIC LEARNER   1

Chapter 1
THE GOOD STRATEGY USER   3
The Successful Learner   4
The Good Strategy User   5
Are You a Good Strategy User?   9
Where Can You Begin?   11
Web Alert!   12

Part 2
KEY STRATEGIES FOR A SMART START   15

Chapter 2
RESOURCES FOR STRATEGIC LEARNERS   17
Start with Your Own Resources   18
Working with Other Students   22
Course Instructors and Outlines   23
Campus Learning Resources   24
Preparing for Your Educational Expedition   28
Web Alert!   29

Chapter 3
ORGANIZING YOUR TIME   30
Managing Time Effectively—A Common Problem   31
Self-Assessment of Current Approach to Time Management   32
A Step-by-Step Time-Management System   33
Recording and Analyzing Time Spent   39
Strategies to Maintain and Enhance Your System   42
Procrastination   43
Understanding Procrastination   44
Remedies for Procrastination   46
What Are Your Suggestions for Time Management?   46
Successful Time Management   48
Web Alert!   48

Chapter 4
LEARNING FROM LECTURES 50
Self-Assessment of Current Approach to Lectures   51
Your Role in the Lecture   52
Listening Strategies   54
Recording Strategies   55
Review Strategies for Lecture Notes   56
Using Abbreviations   57
Graphic Organizers   59
Examples of Strategic Note Taking   60
Suggestions for the Problem Lecture   64
What Are Your Suggestions for Lectures?   65
The Key Role of Lecture Notes   67
Web Alert!   67

Chapter 5
LEARNING FROM TEXTBOOKS 69
Self-Assessment of Current Approach to Academic Reading   70
The Role of the Text in the Course   71
Getting to Know Your Text   72
Set Your Reading Goals   72
SQ4R: A System for Reading Texts   74
Improve Your Reading Efficiency   82
Learn to Skim and Scan   84
What are Your Suggestions for Text Reading?   85
A Personalized Approach to Reading   86
Web Alert!   87

Part 3
GOING BEYOND THE BASICS 89

Chapter 6
EFFECTIVE MEMORY 91
Memory Systems   92
Structuring Information to Enhance Storage   94
Creating Memory Structures   96
An Example of How to Create a Memory Structure   97
Consolidating Information in Long-Term Memory   99
The Crucial Role of Comprehension Monitoring   106
Putting These Ideas to Work   107
Web Alert!   107

Chapter 7
FOCUS ON PROBLEM SOLVING AND LABS 109
Managing Your Problem-Solving Activities   110
Three Key Thinking Strategies   113
Success in the Lab   122

The Day-by-Day Problem Solver   126
Strategies Can Make the Difference   128
Web Alert!   128

Chapter 8

FOCUS ON THE SOCIAL SCIENCES AND HUMANITIES   130
Evaluating Academic Arguments   131
Strategies for Literature Courses   132
Learning a Second Language   141
Diversity of Choice and Strategies   144
Web Alert!   145

Chapter 9

MANAGING THE STRESS OF BEING A STUDENT   146
What Is Stress?   147
Taking Control of Stress   149
Concentration   150
Your Concentration Profile   153
What Are Your Suggestions for Managing Stress?   154
Managing Your Level of Stress   155
Web Alert!   156

Part 4

PUTTING IN A SUCCESSFUL PERFORMANCE   157

Chapter 10

WRITING RESEARCH PAPERS   159
Features of a Good Research Paper   160
Analyzing the Assignment   162
Structure of a Research Paper   163
Stages of Composition   165
Assessing Your Performance   170
Meeting the Challenge   171
Self-Help Books on Effective Writing   171
Web Alert!   172

Chapter 11

CLASS PRESENTATIONS AND SEMINARS   173
Your Attitude to Class Presentations and Seminars   174
Researching the Information   175
Structuring Your Presentation   176
Presenting to the Class   177
Keeping Calm with Visual Imagery   181
Contributing to a Group Presentation   182
Putting It All Together   183
Web Alert!   184

Chapter 12
PREPARING FOR EXAMS   185
Self-Assessment of Current Approach to Exam Preparation   186
Important Steps in Exam Preparation   187
Understanding the Design of Exam Questions: Bloom's Taxonomy   192
Common Review Techniques to Avoid   194
Final Exams   195
What Are Your Suggestions for Exam Preparation?   197
Active, Not Passive, Review   199
Web Alert!   199

Chapter 13
WRITING EXAMS   201
Multiple-Choice Exams   202
Essay Exams   207
Short-Answer Exams   211
Problem-Solving Exams   212
Case-Study Exams   213
Exam Anxiety—Good or Bad?   215
Strategies to Control Exam Anxiety   215
What Are Your Suggestions for Writing Exams?   218
Taking Control of the Exam Situation   219
Web Alert!   220

Index   221

PREFACE

Learning for Success: Effective Strategies for Students, Fourth Edition, is written for students at college and university and in Grade 12 who want to explore effective study methods for achieving maximum academic performance. The unifying theme throughout the book is the model of the Good Strategy User, as we invite you to think about and select those learning strategies that work best for your own learning style and situation.

This fourth edition retains much of what students and counsellors have told us they found useful in previous editions; in addition, chapters have been extensively revised to address new ideas and technology for student learning. A new chapter has been added with a specific focus on the social sciences and humanities; the chapter on effective memory explains how memory structures are a key to academic success; suggestions for working in groups have been added to the chapter on class presentations and seminars; and self-assessment inventories and worksheets have been expanded and clarified as important tools in self-directed learning. In general, revisions clarify and expand upon important concepts and effective learning strategies. Finally, we have given the book a whole new look that we hope you will find attractive and easier to read.

THE MAIN GOALS FOR THIS BOOK
- To increase your awareness as a self-directed learner.
- To introduce to you many specific strategies to improve your academic success.
- To help you incorporate new and effective learning strategies into your own personal approach to learning.
- To suggest that *you* control many of the factors affecting how well you do in school.
- To provide you with a sound and comprehensive self-help resource that you can turn to any time you need to think about and adapt your approach to a specific learning task.

ASSESS YOUR LEARNING STYLE

An important first step in learning "how to learn better" is to spend some time thinking about how you currently approach learning; so, we encourage you to do this now. The more you understand yourself as a learner, the better the choices you can make to reach your full academic potential. For example: What is your main academic goal at this time? What is your favourite subject area? Which academic tasks do you most enjoy? What learning settings work best for you? What do you regard as your strengths as a learner? When have you felt most satisfied with the results of your hard work?

It may well be that you have had most success in the past when the way in which you approached an academic task matched with your preferred learning style. Your "learning style" is your approach to learning when it has become the consistent way in which you try to understand new ideas. The idea of learning styles has been around for a long time. Consequently, there are many different models of learning styles, some simple and some complex. Here, we are going to look at a practical model of learning styles that focuses on how you engage your senses in learning.

The Auditory Learner

This learner learns best by hearing something. He particularly enjoys lectures, never missing one, and while listening to the lecture he maintains an ongoing internal dialogue with the teacher. He gets a lot out of discussion classes, and so he always joins in any study groups that are set up for his courses. He often reads text aloud to himself, and sometimes makes taped summaries and replays them to reinforce the text information.

The Visual Learner

This student learns best by seeing something. In class, she pays particular attention to the overheads, making sure to copy them down in her own notes. Text reading works very well for her, especially if the text is well structured and there are useful diagrams and illustrations. If she works in a group, she needs to write things down, either in her notebook or on a chalkboard or chart. For review she makes organized charts and summaries of the main points, and she visualizes a lot of practical examples to illustrate any abstract concepts.

The Tactile/Kinesthetic Learner

This learner learns best when he can be an active participant. He always enjoys and does well in any lab or studio component. If he has the opportunity, he opts for co-op classes. To fit with his style, he will go to the gym, and at the same time he will think through some of the academic tasks he has to accomplish, such as reinforcing information for a test or planning his approach to a research paper.

WHAT WORKS BEST FOR YOU?

For the academic tasks below, what would be your first, most preferred, approach for each? Circle just one response for each task: a, b, or c.

1. You have to make a decision about choosing a new course for next term:
   a. You talk to your friends, parents, and teachers about your options.
   b. You take time to think about your options, reading through course descriptions and trying to picture the kinds of content each course will cover.

    c. You look through course descriptions and talk to people about how much practical or hands-on experience each course will require.

2. You have just moved into the student residence, and you set out to find your way around:

    a. You ask other students and staff about the facilities in the residence.

    b. You check through the literature you were given to find a map that shows the layout of the building.

    c. You go out and explore, creating a mental map as you go.

3. You are setting up a weekly schedule to organize your study time:

    a. You talk to your best friend to find out what works for her.

    b. You draw a weekly schedule, and then add in your classes and other commitments.

    c. You check out some locations on campus that might work well for your studying.

4. You are in class, concentrating on the lecture:

    a. You listen to your teacher for clues, such as repetition or emphasis, to the most important information.

    b. You pay particular attention to anything the teacher illustrates with diagrams or overheads and make sure to take notes.

    c. You watch the teacher's body language for clues to key points.

5. You are working on remembering the main ideas you selected out of your text reading:

    a. You get together with a friend, and you test each other.

    b. You make a chart that organizes the main ideas.

    c. You mentally recite the main ideas as you go for your evening jog.

6. You are preparing for your weekly chemistry lab:

    a. You read the instructions out loud to yourself.

    b. You read over your lab handout, highlighting the main points in the lab manual and visualizing the equipment that you have to set up.

    c. You go into the lab to check out the apparatus you will be using.

7. You are just beginning to research a major paper:

    a. You talk to your professor to check that you are clear about the criteria and your topic.

    b. You think about the subject area and some possible topics, and for each you jot down some examples to try to map out your approach.

c. You go for a walk, thinking through the questions that can help direct your enquiry. You write them down when you get home.

8. You have a major test next week:
   a. You attend a group review session and ask questions about content that you are unsure of.
   b. You make a reduced set of study notes, making sure to include many examples.
   c. You find an empty classroom and use the chalkboard to summarize key ideas.

Evaluating Your Learning Style

Total your a, b, and c responses, and fill in the numbers in the table below:

	a Auditory	b Visual	c Tactile/ Kinesthetic
Total	4	2	2

For these eight learning tasks, which of the three senses do you favour: auditory, visual, or tactile/kinesthetic? You may find that one sense predominates or that you take a more balanced approach.

In each chapter of this book, you will find many suggested learning strategies to help you reach your academic goals. You are not expected to use them all. First of all, choose to try those new strategies that best fit your preferred learning style. **As a learner, however, it is not always possible to get an exact match between an academic task and your preferred learning style.** A specific task may dictate how it is to be done and require that you take a broader approach. This is when you need to explore alternative strategies that can lead to your success. Knowing this can help you to plan additional time for the task and find creative ways to handle it. When trying any new strategies, remember to give them time to work, as it takes a certain amount of time and effort to build in new approaches to make your learning more efficient and successful.

LEARNING SKILLS ON THE WEB

At the end of each chapter in this book, Web links direct you to sites that expand upon selected ideas. The Web is a very dynamic medium, and Web page addresses change, so we have mainly selected links to universities and colleges as their main addresses will likely be current even if a link to a specific Web page has been discontinued. As this book is specifically written for Canadian students, we have included learning skills Web pages from many Canadian universities and colleges.

Carefully type Web addresses, as mistakes are easily made and connections then can't go through. If after checking that the address is entered correctly you find that a Web page is no longer active, go to the home page of the institution by putting in just the first part of the address. Then follow internal links or use their search engines to locate learning resources of interest.

WEB ALERT!

Mount Saint Vincent University
Halifax, Nova Scotia
www.msvu.ca/student_affairs/StudySkills/reasonexercise.asp
An exercise of three questions exploring reasons for attending university.

Conestoga College
Kitchener, Ontario
www.conestogac.on.ca/jsp/stserv/learningstrategies/index.jsp
Follow the link on this Learning Strategies introductory page to "Learning Styles." This will take you to "About Learning Styles," "Learning Style Inventory," and "Characteristics."

Durham College
Oshawa, Ontario, Canada
www.durhamcollege.ca/EN/main/students/17638/student_success.php
Compares high school and college and provides a comprehensive set of tips for becoming a successful student.

ACKNOWLEDGMENTS

We would like to acknowledge the contribution of the many students and colleagues who continue to share their experiences with us and provide support and encouragement for *Learning for Success*. We also appreciate the many people at Thomson Nelson who have worked on this edition of the book, including Michael Thompson, Rebecca Rea, Kelli Howey, and Julie van Veen for all of their efforts and encouragement. Last but not least, we thank our families, and most especially Alexandra Zajchowski, Michael Fleet, and Michael Goodchild. Without the interest and support of many people, this project would not have been possible.

PHOTO CREDITS

Chapter 1 Diversity Lifestyles Disc © Comstock; Chapter 2 © Chuck Savage/CORBIS/Magma; Chapter 3 Dick Hemingway; Chapter 4 Dick Hemingway; Chapter 5 Dick Hemingway; Chapter 6 Steve Dunwell/Image Bank/Getty Images; Chapter 7 Jochen Eckel/DPA/Landov; Chapter 8 © Spencer Grant/Photo Edit; Chapter 9 Dick Hemingway; Chapter 10 Photodisc; Chapter 11 © Colin Young-Wolff/Photo Edit; Chapter 12 © Bill Varie/CORBIS/Magma; Chapter 13 Photodisc.

Part 1

HOW TO BE A STRATEGIC LEARNER

Chapter 1

THE GOOD STRATEGY USER

LEARNING OBJECTIVES

The purpose of this chapter is for you to:
- Read about the unifying theme of this book—the Good Strategy User.
- Recognize that adequate background knowledge is essential for academic success.
- Think about the importance of your attitudes and beliefs about learning.
- Explore two types of strategies: self-management and thinking strategies.
- Rate yourself as a Good Strategy User.

L earning is such a complex process that we no longer try to explain a student's progress simplistically by just saying that the student is naturally bright, average, or poor. Although a student's natural ability is an important component of his or her academic success, other factors such as home background and experiences, personality, formal schooling, motivation, and persistence also contribute greatly to the student's performance. In addition, successful students, regardless of any other factors, typically apply effective learning strategies to their tasks. While students may not have been able to control all the factors that have affected their past academic progress, they can take charge of the current learning strategies that they choose to apply. The focus of this book, therefore, is on the use of learning strategies.

A learning strategy is a specific approach to a learning task that you choose to use to improve your learning effectiveness. Sitting down each evening to list tasks to be done and then planning times to work on them is an example of a time-management strategy. There are, of course, many strategies that you can use in each of the areas of learning: time management, learning from lectures, exam preparation, and so on. If you have a system for organizing your thinking about your own strategy use, then making decisions on which strategies to use is made much easier. The Good Strategy User model[1] introduced in this chapter and used throughout this book provides you with such a structured system. This model presents four components for you to consider when making academic choices: your background knowledge, your attitudes and beliefs, two types of strategies that you apply, and your ability to control and make necessary changes to your current approach.

THE SUCCESSFUL LEARNER

Melanie is a first-year student who has just received a test result in her introductory history course. She can't wait to get back to residence to share the great news with her roommate Karen that her very first test mark is an A.

Karen responds just as Melanie expects: with a wild yell, and she dances around the room. Then she flops down on the bed and says, "You know, I'm not at all surprised that you got that A because . . . "

1. _you are very smart and studied hard and knew your material._

_____

2. _studied hard_

3. _knew your material_

How do you think that Karen is explaining Melanie's success? Can you fill in some of the reasons why Melanie's mark was an A? Try to list at least three reasons before reading further.

THE GOOD STRATEGY USER

While some might argue that the two main reasons for Melanie's A are that Melanie is very bright and that she works hard, the Good Strategy User model suggests that Melanie's performance in school was greatly enhanced through her appropriate use of learning strategies.

Let us take a closer look at four components that contributed to Melanie's effective strategy use: her background knowledge, her personal attitudes toward and beliefs about school, her specific learning strategies, and her awareness of her own strategy use. As you read, think about your own academic performance. How does each one of these four components contribute to your academic success?

BACKGROUND KNOWLEDGE

Melanie took history every year in high school, so this introductory course does not contain too many surprises. For example, the struggles between the French and English settlers in Canada are not new to her, although never before has she gone into such detailed analysis of the Acadian deportation. Her previous history courses provided Melanie with an adequate background, so she seldom feels overwhelmed or lost in class. In addition, she prepares for each class by reading ahead in the text. She knows that she gets a lot more out of a lecture when she has done her homework thoroughly and has a sound knowledge base of the current topic.

If you are to be a Good Strategy User, you need a knowledge base that is at least minimally adequate for a course. You may not always be able to select courses for which you have a very extensive base of knowledge, but your level of knowledge should be such that you are not constantly struggling to keep your head above water. An inadequate knowledge base in one course can lead to an overly demanding workload, which can sabotage your efforts in other courses by leaving you with too little study time for them.

PERSONAL ATTITUDES AND BELIEFS

Melanie takes responsibility for her own learning, and this is reflected in her attitudes and beliefs about learning. If a lecture is hard to follow or a concept is very challenging, Melanie maintains a positive attitude and looks for a way to deal with the problem. She avoids blaming external factors such as her instructor or the course. Melanie believes that she will succeed in her studies if she plans her activities and chooses appropriate strategies to meet important goals. She is also a firm believer in both working and playing hard, and so she does not feel guilty taking time out to play squash, knowing that she has planned for that.

Attitudes

A positive attitude—to being a student, to school, to classmates, to courses and programs—is a major contributor to success. A positive attitude translates into motivation, enthusiasm, and energy to do work, and with it you are more likely to take a thoughtful, strategic approach to studying. As soon as you tell yourself that you do not like being in school or that you do not like a specific course, you have made your situation much more difficult. If you can find ways to make your courses enjoyable even when faced with some difficulties, it is much more likely that you will succeed.

Beliefs

Beliefs that you hold about yourself as a learner as well as various aspects of school can have a major influence on your use of study strategies. For example, if you believe that you always take a long time to learn a concept or that multiple-choice tests are out to trick you, then you will be much less likely to put in any real effort and will be less likely to improve and succeed in these areas. Beliefs can be resistant to change because they have often developed over a long period of time. It is important to evaluate beliefs that you hold about your potential to succeed and then to work on any negative beliefs that you feel are blocking your progress.

LEARNING STRATEGIES

Reading the text before class is one specific strategy that works for Melanie. Applying such learning strategies to tasks is crucial to good strategy use. Unfortunately, many students confuse general good intentions (e.g., working harder or managing time better) with strategies. Good intentions rarely translate into effective action unless they are rephrased as specific strategies. Melanie, for example, realizes that to succeed in her courses she will have to put in sufficient and effective study time. Melanie has worked out a number of strategies for ensuring that she achieves this good intention, so she has made a plan for studying that has 20 hours of study time each week, and she has included time to review her class notes briefly each day.

Rephrase each of the following good intentions into a specific learning strategy:

1. "I will take better lecture notes."

   Listen for ideas repeated. Listen for cues, such as "this is a possible midterm question."

2. "I will do a better job of preparing for tests."

   Review text before class. Review lecture notes briefly after every class

If you have trouble translating these two good intentions into specific learning strategies, refer to the relevant strategies in Chapter 4, "Learning from Lectures," and Chapter 12, "Preparing for Exams," and then come back to complete the exercise.

It is useful to recognize two major types of learning strategies, both of which are essential to academic success. One type, strategies for self-management, enables Melanie to take control of her learning environment. Melanie applies the second type, thinking strategies, as she works with and processes course content.

Self-Management Strategies

Melanie manages the environment in which she studies:

- She has a favourite quiet corner in the library, and she chooses to go there to read the history text.
- She chooses to sit where the lighting is just right so her eyes do not get tired.
- She sets herself a goal of reading ten text pages before taking a short break.

Strategies for self-management set the environment for study and are important steps to accomplishing learning goals. For a given academic goal, you need to decide where you will study, how you will set up your study environment, and for how long you will study that material.

Keep in mind factors such as lighting, comfort and convenience of the furniture, ventilation, and potential distractions. Plan to have all necessary materials at hand, especially if you are working away from your own room. For optimum concentration, schedule your meals so that you are not hungry or too full as you study. Think carefully about what you will wear, as you do not want to be physically uncomfortable while you study.

You need to consider the best times to accomplish certain tasks. For example, it may suit you best to work on math problems in the morning and read the novels for your Canadian literature course in the evening. The Good Strategy User is aware of the best times for academic tasks. Strategic use of resources also affects the quality of your learning environment. In addition to consultations with your instructors, there may be other important resources available such as writing and counselling centres and computer facilities. Get started early in using all the resources available to you. With effective self-management strategies, you create a learning environment that makes the most of your learning experience.

Thinking Strategies

Melanie is strategic as she thinks about course content:

- As she listens to the lecture she consciously listens for themes, and she includes subtitles in her notes to label them.
- Melanie makes time to reread her lecture notes after class, checks that she understands all the main ideas, and adds key words to the margins of her notes to summarize these main ideas.
- If she does not understand something in the lecture, Melanie works to clarify the problem by consulting her text, asking another student, or checking with her instructor.

If you are to understand new ideas and learn them in such a way that you can remember and apply the ideas to new situations, you need effective thinking strategies for learning, consolidating, and applying information. These thinking strategies are not just a matter of luck. If you are to be a successful student, you will plan the strategies you apply to your studies.

Three important goals to guide your planning of thinking strategies are:

1. To have good comprehension of the key ideas.
2. To have a good memory of the information.
3. To be able to apply the knowledge to new situations.

As you study, it is useful to ask yourself questions that will help you achieve these three goals: "Does this make sense to me? How does this new information relate to concepts that we covered previously in this course? How will I be tested on this information?" Asking questions is an important thinking strategy. As you read this book, you will be asked to consider using many strategies that encourage you to think about how you learn new information. Chapter 6, "Effective Memory," explores some very important thinking strategies that will enhance long-term retention of essential information.

STRATEGIC AWARENESS

Strategic awareness refers to Melanie's knowledge about her own learning style and her ability to coordinate appropriate learning strategies. So, Melanie not only has strategies at her disposal, but also knows a lot about which are the best strategies to use for a particular task; that is, when, where, and how to use them. For example, when Melanie prepared for this history test, she thought about and planned the specific learning strategies she would use. Knowing that she was primarily a visual learner, she decided to use a graphic organizer to summarize the major events covered by the test, and so she drew a timeline and used colour to highlight the sequence of events. Because this test included short-answer questions, and Melanie predicted that she would need to know specific place names, she devised a mnemonic (memory-aiding) device—in this case, an acronym that she wrote down—to help her remember key locations. When Melanie felt that she was prepared for this short-answer test, she practised recalling key information from memory by jotting points down on some scrap paper. Strategies have to be appropriate to the style of the learner and the learning task if they are to be effective, and Melanie devised preparation strategies specific to her learning style and to the content and style of this test.

As a Good Strategy User, you need to be reflective about your preferred learning style and learning strategies. Think about the following questions: Are you able to identify your learning skills strengths? Do you take into account your learning style when you choose strategies? Do you have knowledge of alternative approaches you might take to reviewing for tests? Flexibility of approach is a central characteristic of the Good Strategy User, and the more knowledgeable you are about learning strategies, the better you can coordinate them to meet study demands.

ARE YOU A GOOD STRATEGY USER?

How do you rate yourself as a Good Strategy User? Choose one course that you are currently taking, and think about your learning style together with the four components of the model.

Name of course: *Records Management*

Your preferred learning style (see Preface): *Auditory*

1. How and when did you acquire your background knowledge for this course, and is it adequate for you to keep up with the course material without too much difficulty?

   I took a 3hr book training course 2 yrs ago, It is pretty easy to keep up.

2. How would you describe your general attitude to this course, and what do you believe about your potential to do well in this course?

   I feel it is a course I can master once I totally understand the rules. First class mark is what I am aiming for (ie. A range).

3. Specify one effective self-management strategy and one thinking strategy that you apply to this course when learning new information. How do these strategies reflect your preferred learning style?

   Strategy for self-management:

   Using agenda to plan at least a few days in advance

   Strategy for thinking about new academic information:

   Hands-on experience

4. Give examples of some alternatives available to you in adapting your strategic approach to reading a text chapter if you are very short of time. Keep in mind your learning style as you do this.

   Focus on key points and skim through the common sense parts.

DISCUSSION OF YOUR RESPONSES

1. The importance of background knowledge varies from course to course. Many first-year courses are introductory in nature, and you are not expected to have very much background knowledge at all. However, in advanced courses and in mathematical problem-solving courses it is very important that you have adequate and up-to-date background knowledge. This is why some courses have prerequisites; that is, you must take the prerequisite course before taking the more advanced course. The prerequisite course is a safeguard, ensuring that you have the necessary backgound knowledge you need to be able to succeed. If you do find yourself struggling in a course because you feel you lack background knowledge, it is important that you discuss this situation with your instructor or an academic counsellor as soon as possible.

2. There are a number of questions you might ask yourself about your course. Is the course content interesting and/or relevant to your learning goals? Is your instructor well prepared? Does the class environment foster learning? Hopefully, you are feeling positive about your course. However, if you find that you are holding on to some negative attitudes or beliefs, try to discuss this with someone you feel is both easy to talk to and positive in outlook.

3. There are, of course, many strategies that you could choose both for self-management and for thinking about new information. Look at the strategies that you wrote down, and check that they are specific strategies and not simply good intentions. Do your strategies reflect in some way your preferred learning style? As you read Part 2 of this book, "Key Strategies for a Smart Start," you will learn about many self-management strategies for locating and using resources as well as for successful time management. You will also learn about the many thinking strategies that apply to learning from lectures and from your texts.

4. If you are short of time for reading a text chapter, here are some possible alternatives you could consider: survey the headings carefully, and then think about how the headings are organized and what you already know about the topic; read the chapter summary thoroughly; or ask a fellow classmate who has done the reading to explain the chapter to you (this latter strategy can also be useful to your classmate).

WHERE CAN YOU BEGIN?

Before you move on to the next chapter, one important point needs to be re-emphasized. Study habits can be difficult to change, and it is often easier to take the path of least resistance and stay with the comfortable old ways of doing things. When you are trying out a new strategy, it will take a little time before you begin to use it automatically. You may have to generate ways to remind yourself regularly of this new strategy you are trying to adopt. Also, note that not all strategies work for everyone, and you may see friends studying in a different way from you. Have confidence that you can evaluate your own learning style and needs and choose the strategies that are best for you.

This chapter introduced you to the model of the Good Strategy User, which you can use to help you think about all the factors that have an impact on your learning success. The four components of the Good Strategy User model—background knowledge, personal attitudes and beliefs, learning strategies (for self-management and thinking about new information), and strategic awareness—provide you with a systematic framework for evaluating your current approach to learning. If you are having difficulty in a subject, track through the four components of the Good Strategy User model so that you can pinpoint the source of your problems and identify strategies that can make a difference.

Having introduced you in Part 1 of this book to the idea of strategic learning, the following chapters focus on a wide variety of strategies that cover the major academic tasks that students have to complete. These chapters are organized into three parts: "Key Strategies for a Smart Start," "Going Beyond the Basics," and "Putting in a Successful Performance." As you read each chapter, evaluate the strategies that are presented and concentrate on those that you think can make a difference to the quality of your own study techniques.

w w w WEB ALERT!

University of Canberra
Canberra, Australia
www.canberra.edu.au/studyskills/learning/indlearning.html
Academic Skills Online: Learning Independently

(This is where Dr. Aliron Bielak is doing her Post Doc. in PSYC.)

Selkirk College
Nelson, British Columbia
http://people.selkirk.bc.ca/akosling
Student Services: Study Skills Centres. Click on "Motivation and Attitude" under the Study Skills Links on the left side of the screen

Queen's University
Kingston, Ontario
www.cs.queensu.ca/home/skill/learning.html
Learning Techniques

CHAPTER ENDNOTE

1. The term "Good Strategy User" was first used in "Cognitive Strategies: Good Strategy Users Coordinate Metacognition and Knowledge," by M. Pressley, J. G. Borkowski, & W. Schneider, 1987, *Annals of Child Development, 4,* pp. 89–129.

Part 2

KEY STRATEGIES FOR A SMART START

Chapter 2

RESOURCES FOR STRATEGIC LEARNERS

LEARNING OBJECTIVES

The purpose of this chapter is for you to:

- Make some key personal decisions for the start of the school year.
- Think about the advantages of working with other students.
- Consider the importance of getting help from your instructor.
- Learn how to use your course outlines to your advantage.
- Check out campus resources that support your academic success.

The first few weeks of any new term can be a challenge, especially if you are making that major transition from one school to another. With so many people to meet, things to find out about, and decisions to make, you need to apply quickly some excellent strategies if you are to get off to a "Smart Start." The chapter you have just read introduced the idea of your becoming a Good Strategy User. This current chapter and the three that follow continue that idea of strategy development as they cover key components of the learning experience that you need to have in place as early in the term as possible. This chapter explores self-management strategies to apply to resources that support your learning efforts; the following three chapters explore time management and learning from lectures and texts.

START WITH YOUR OWN RESOURCES

Before or shortly after your courses begin, think about and make key personal decisions relating to your academic program and course choices, your academic goals, and your study environment.

YOUR ACADEMIC PROGRAM AND COURSE CHOICES

As you start your academic year, be as well informed as possible about your chosen academic program and all of the courses you have selected to take. Hopefully, you are happy with your choices. However, it is not uncommon for some students to rethink and make some changes at the start of the academic year, and most schools have a limited add/drop time period during which such changes can be made if space in programs and classes allows—and, of course, if the students are eligible to do so. So if you are not satisfied with any of your initial decisions, and you want to make some changes, check out the rules and regulations so that you know what you have to do and where you go to do it.

- Study your academic calendar carefully, especially for deadlines and locations for adding and dropping courses. The sooner you make necessary changes, the less negative impact there will be. You do not want to miss those crucial first lectures. If you do make changes, be careful to understand all possible implications. Are you closing doors to opportunities that you might later regret? Will the changes affect your academic status, current level of funding, or funding source?
- If you do need to make any changes to your chosen program or courses, seek out the academic advisers at your institution. Their role is to answer your questions, help you to understand all of the requirements, point out any restrictions or problems with changes you want to make, and make sure that you are fully informed on any implications for the future.

- When you make program and course choices, you should follow your own interests and instincts that this is the correct path for you. You can sometimes make poor choices because of pressure from others, especially peer pressure. Always remember that the final choice is yours, and you must feel comfortable with it.

YOUR ACADEMIC GOALS

The beginning of a new term is the right time to think about and start applying goal-setting strategies. Without clear academic goals, you may just drift along until suddenly you realize that tests are looming and assignments are due, and you have to scramble. By getting into the habit of setting goals at the start of the school year, you can avoid these nasty surprises later on. Think about two types of academic goals: long-term and short-term.

Long-term Goals

If you are not clear on your long-term academic goals, you may have difficulty staying motivated to work toward them on a day-to-day basis. One student told us that at the beginning of each year, he would write down in the front of each of his new textbooks the reasons for his taking each course. He said that if he found his enthusiasm for a class flagging, he would re-read his own words, and they would always help to recharge his energy for the course. So, at the beginning of a new school year, you need to think about your long-term academic goals. Long-term goals are global in scope. Take a look at our examples, and then write down four long-term academic goals that you are aiming to achieve:

- I plan to graduate on time for my program along with all of my classmates.
- I am aiming to get at least a B+ average this year.
- One of my academic goals this year is to learn a new language, so I have registered for a Spanish class.
- I want to improve my writing skills, so have already made an appointment at the Student Learning Centre to see the writing specialist.

My Long-term Goals:

1. _____

   _____

2. _____

   _____

3. _____

_____

4. _____

_____

_____

Short-term Goals

Short-term goals are the immediate and specific academic goals that can help you make the most of each and every day, eventually adding up to the achievement of those long-term goals that you set for yourself. In developing the skill of setting short-term goals and applying them strategically, you need to recognize the important difference between **content-oriented** and **strategy-oriented** short-term goals. Content-oriented goals specify the task you have to do, while strategy-oriented goals specify the approach you will take. In addition, short-term content-oriented and strategy-oriented goals should always be accompanied by a **time-management** goal.

For a content-oriented goal, ask yourself, "**What** do I plan to get done right now?" Your answer might be, "I plan to finish ten math problems." In contrast, for the strategy-oriented goal for this same task, you would ask, "**How** shall I proceed with this task?" Your answer might be, "I will first of all review my class notes, then re-do the solved examples, and then I will attempt the new problems." For your time-management goal, ask yourself, "**How long** do I plan to give to this task?" One of the aims of this book is to help you become a more successful student by setting all three types of short-term goals. Begin by setting short-term goals for two of today's academic tasks:

My Short-Term Goals:

1. The first academic task I have to get done is:

_____

This is how I intend to proceed:

_____

_____

I plan to spend this amount of time to complete this task:

_____

2. The second academic task I have to get done is:

_____

This is how I intend to proceed:

_____

_____

I plan to spend this amount of time to complete this task:

_____

Consider the following principles for setting short-term goals:

1. *Set goals that are specific and measurable:* for example, "Over the next hour, I will start my research paper for History 101 by creating a working outline and brainstorming a few points for each of the subtopics."
2. *Set goals that are positive and realistic:* for example, "I will read this anthropology chapter in two-page chunks then summarize the main ideas, and I aim to spend the next two hours on this task."
3. *Plan ways to remind yourself of the goals you have set:* for example, "I will write down my goals for today in my day planner."
4. *Share your goals with people who have an impact on your study patterns and space:* for example, "I will be working in my room for the next hour, as I need some undisturbed time to work on my math quiz for tomorrow."
5. *Establish rewards for the completion of your goals:* for example, "I will watch my favourite TV show tonight when I have finished my planned study tasks."

YOUR STUDY ENVIRONMENT

At the beginning of the school year, decide where you are going to study on a regular basis. A **good study location** can make all the difference. It is likely that your main study space will be your own room in residence or at home. If you have to share your space with a roommate, you will have to find alternative study locations for those times when quiet study is essential. You may find that a favourite corner of the library works best for you.

You will need **ready access to a computer,** as so many resources are available online:

- You can find course information on websites dedicated to your courses.
- You can check the locations and hours of operation of any services you need to use.

- You can check if materials are in the library, place a hold on a book, and actively research your institution's online resources.
- You can access information through the Web on many key issues that you might be researching in class.

You will also need a computer to complete assignments, but a few words of warning are in order here to protect your work. Save your file regularly when working on your computer, always print off a hard copy, and make sure to back up key files. Be smart and recognize that computers can be very addictive! It is important to limit time that you spend on non-academic activities: e-mail, chat rooms, and generally surfing the Web. You can waste a lot of time that could otherwise be used for studying.

Your personal study environment should have a **reliable and organized filing system**. You will be taking a lot of notes in class and from readings, generating assignments, and having tests returned. All of this means that you will be handling a lot of paper over the school year, and so you need to be strategic in setting up an adequate filing system at the beginning of the year that you can adapt as the year proceeds. The type of system you choose will depend on your preferences as well as on the demands of courses you take. Consider using loose-leaf binders, so that for each course you can include handouts, returned tests, and so on, all in the same binder. Whatever system you choose, it should be one in which you can readily store and efficiently find course materials.

WORKING WITH OTHER STUDENTS[1]

You will be meeting many other students during the course of the year, and you may choose to spend some of your study time with another student or as part of a group. Meeting other students is an integral part of your education, not just for social connections but as a way to enrich your learning. Studying with others can help to motivate you and improve your ability to work as a team player. You can help each other in a variety of ways, such as reminding one another of upcoming tests or changes to the course schedule, discussing the difficulty of a particular assignment, sharing notes, or suggesting other resources.

Find out if your institution sets up any study groups, as they may be organized for individual courses or in the residences. If not, ask around among your friends and classmates to see if they are interested in starting a study group. There are several key elements to consider if a study group is to benefit all of its members:

1. Groups need to take on tasks that can benefit from the input of a number of different students. Although discussion about the whole project takes place at the group level, individual students take responsibility for specific parts of the task:
   - For a group class presentation, each student can prepare one subtopic to present to the class.
   - For a joint lab report, each student can write up one section of the report.
   - When reviewing for a test, each student can take responsibility for reviewing a few key concepts and can predict a number of questions that might be on the test related to those concepts.
   - Other similar tasks for groups to tackle include discussion of case studies, brainstorming for essay topics, and mathematical problem solving in courses such as math, physics, chemistry, and economics.
2. Each group member needs to agree on specifics such as scheduling, location, and assignment of tasks. Keep in mind that the workload of group members should be equitable, as groups fall apart quickly if some members are freeloading and not contributing to the group.
3. Group members should recognize their responsibility to others in the group by respecting the input of others, focusing on the task at hand, keeping to deadlines, and producing a quality end product.

COURSE INSTRUCTORS AND OUTLINES

Your course instructors are valuable learning resources. At first, you may feel a little intimidated to speak to them, especially if you are in large classes, but instructors can provide you with the help you need if you meet them during their office hours or by appointment. By preparing fairly specific questions ahead of time, you increase the likelihood that your instructor will provide the help you need.

The course outline provided by your instructor is a valuable learning resource, as it is a road map for the plan and direction of the course. At the beginning of the term, check each course outline for the following:

☑ your instructor's name, office location, and office hours
☑ the course objectives and your instructor's approach to assignments and exams
☑ a topic outline for lectures and a listing of required readings
☑ the method of evaluation in the course, including how marks are to be allotted

☑ any special instructions about how to complete assignments, papers, labs, etc.

☑ additional learning resources such as help centres or tutors

Key Contacts for My Courses

INSTRUCTOR'S NAME	OFFICE HOURS AND LOCATION	TELEPHONE	E-MAIL

CAMPUS LEARNING RESOURCES

Find out about the many resources that your school provides to support student learning. If you are new to campus, treat yourself to a guided tour; if one is not available, maybe you can talk a senior student into showing you around. If even that is not available and you are on your own, pick up a campus map and explore. In addition to providing services related to admissions, registration, housing, parking, and financial aid, many institutions provide specific resources to support your learning efforts and personal and social well-being.

First-year Programs/Orientation Sessions

If your campus has a special program for first-year students, be sure to check it out *before* beginning your courses. Generally it will include an orientation tour of the campus, especially all of those resources that can contribute to student success. At some institutions orientation activities are provided by counselling services, student council, or the libraries. They will be well advertised, so be on the lookout for them. They provide opportunities for you to learn a lot about the campus in a small amount of time.

Learning Skills Counselling

You can usually find at least one counsellor on campus whose main function is to help students learn more efficiently. Typically, learning skills counsellors offer presentations or workshops on learning strategies for tasks such as lecture note taking, text reading, time management, and exam preparation and writing. The counsellor may offer diagnostic tests to check your strategy use or evaluate your learning style. You can talk one-on-one to this counsellor about any academic problems you are experiencing, such as poor concentration or test anxiety. You do not have to be failing a course to use the learning skills services. If you are interested in improving your learning strategies, this is the person to talk to—whatever your grades.

Help Centres

There may be a centralized Student Learning Centre and/or centres located in academic departments or faculties; for example, the Writing Centre, the Biology Help Centre, or the Math Centre. A learning centre may have examples of old exams, tutorial worksheets, tapes and videos, and a wide variety of handouts and instructions for key topics. Often learning centres employ many part-time staff, so meet as many as possible and find the one or two individuals with whom you can work best. Use the centre regularly to clear up difficulties with your studies as they arise.

Services for Students with Disabilities

Campuses provide services for students with disabilities so they can find key information about available services and arrange for accommodations. Institutions vary widely in what services are provided and accommodations allowed. If you are planning to use these services, make an appointment with a counsellor as early as possible, preferably well before the term begins. You will want to find out about the options available to you before you finalize your course choices.

LIBRARIES

Take a guided tour, if possible, to find out about the layouts of the buildings, the location of certain collections, the catalogue system, and how to access services. Pick up handouts that describe the library and its many resources; often, there are handouts for specific disciplines listing up-to-date databases available. You will be able to access many of the library resources from your computer at home, and this can save a lot of time when you are researching topics. You will find that you can access the resources of many libraries all over the world from your computer.

TUTORING SERVICES

If you run into serious difficulties with a course, you may wish to use tutoring services. Check with your academic department for names of recommended tutors. Think carefully about your expectations for a tutor, as there are many misconceptions among students about the role of tutors. A tutor is there to clarify areas that you are unsure about—not to teach you all of the information. For example, if you have a tutor to help you with a physics course, you will need to go through your lecture notes to identify sections that are unclear to you; you will have to attempt some of the assigned problems to find those places where you get stuck. The tutor is there to help you after you have defined your problems.

SELF-HELP BOOKS

This book that you are reading is a good example of a self-help book that encourages you to examine and improve your approach to learning. There are many books on the market on specific aspects of studying, such as writing research papers and test taking, so check your campus bookstore for the most up-to-date titles.

OMBUDSPERSON

The ombudsperson acts as a mediator for students who are experiencing serious problems with the school, college, or university. For example, if you have a difficult problem related to university regulations and policies or to academic issues, or you have a concern about a housing or residence issue that is interfering with your ability to manage your studies, talk to the ombudsperson. You will receive helpful advice on your problem as well as suggestions on dealing with it.

CAREER RESOURCE CENTRE

The Career Resource Centre is often one of the busiest spots on campus as students explore the exciting world of work and careers. The services provided are usually very broad, supporting both career development and job search. Career development is that stage of investigating, exploring, and making decisions about the kind of career that you would like. Job search usually includes activities such as writing résumés and cover letters, practising interview skills, networking, and seeking out and applying for job opportunities. You can usually talk with an individual counsellor, attend group presentations and workshops, and use self-help resources in the Career Resource Centre.

VOLUNTEERING

Many institutions are expanding volunteer opportunities on campus and in local communities. They are recognizing the importance of volunteering, to both those who receive the services and those who provide them. Give serious thought to becoming a volunteer if you are looking for opportunities that can benefit others and, at the same time, provide you with opportunities to put into practise and further develop the knowledge and skills you are learning as a student. The Student Learning Centre or the Career Resource Centre may be the places to look for volunteer opportunities, or your institution may have a unit specifically for that purpose.

OTHER CAMPUS RESOURCES

There are other campus resources in addition to those that primarily support your academic success. Be a Good Strategy User and find out about what is available and, if appropriate to your needs, make good use of the following:

- The chaplain's office
- The international students' office
- Offices for students from minority groups
- Personal counselling
- Student health services
- Students' council and clubs

Four Campus Resources That I Plan to Use This Year

RESOURCE	LOCATION	MAIN BENEFITS TO ME

PREPARING FOR YOUR EDUCATIONAL EXPEDITION

At the beginning of an academic year, you can anticipate some of the academic challenges that will be part of your educational journey. Finding support resources is not always easy because they may be numerous and scattered, especially in colleges and universities. As well, resources may not always be well advertised, so you may have to seek them out.

This chapter looked at the many academic resources available to you as a student as you make a smart start to the school year. It began by focusing on some of the key personal decisions you need to make. The chapter then moved outward to working with other students and making the most of your instructors as a resource. Finally, it outlined the array of campus learning resources that can help you on your educational journey. Chapter 3, "Organizing Your Time," continues the theme of self-management strategies by taking a close look at one of the most important issues to fall within your personal control: time management.

WEB ALERT!

Concordia University
Montreal, Quebec
http://cdev.concordia.ca/CnD/studentlearn/Help/handouts/Learning/smartchoices.HO
Smart Choices for Learning: Study Skills for the New Student

University of Victoria
Victoria, British Columbia
www.coun.uvic.ca/learn/program/hndouts/smartgoals.html
Learning Skills Program: Smart Goals

Southern Illinois University Edwardsville
Edwardsville, Illinois
www.siue.edu/SPIN/activity.html
A Goal Setting Model for Academic Success—published by the Learning and Study Skills Spin Group of NADE (National Association for Developmental Education)

Your Own Institution
Find and fill in the main Web address for your school:

_____

Follow internal links to four student resources important to you. Record their Web addresses.

1. _____

2. _____

3. _____

4. _____

CHAPTER ENDNOTE

1. For more information on working in groups, check out pages 182–183 in Chapter 11, "Class Presentations and Seminars."

Chapter 3

ORGANIZING YOUR TIME

LEARNING OBJECTIVES

The purpose of this chapter is for you to:
- Check your present experience with time management.
- Learn about five steps to effective time management.
- Apply these steps to your own learning situation.
- Apply strategies to maintain and enhance your time-management system.
- Learn about examples of and reasons for procrastination.
- Select strategies that you can use to overcome procrastination.

Time management is a fact of life for everyone, although there are many differences in how individuals make choices about how to organize their time. For some people, time management is little more than responding to things that happen. Others are rigid controllers with definite plans at all times. However, the majority of us are located somewhere in between these two extremes, with many wishing for a more consistent ability to achieve a balance between school and leisure and work commitments.

This chapter invites you to assess your current time-management strategies, because raising your personal awareness is an important first step to taking control of your time. Then it introduces you to a step-by-step time-management system including strategies for maintaining and enhancing your basic plan. Finally, it looks at the reasons behind procrastination and suggests ways to avoid it. By applying the suggested self-management strategies, you can achieve better academic results and enjoy your leisure time without feeling guilty. That's what successful time management is all about.

MANAGING TIME EFFECTIVELY—A COMMON PROBLEM

My friend dropped by last night, and I didn't like to tell him that I had a lot of work to do.

I belong to a couple of clubs, but I find it tough fitting them in with my course load and my part-time job.

It takes me many hours to do all the required reading for my weekly history tutorial.

I work really hard, but I never seem to get everything done that I should.

Practices for the football team are at 4:00 p.m. each day, and I don't get home until 7:00 p.m. By the time I finish my supper, I am ready for a nap.

Students commonly report problems like those above. They find it a challenge to handle unexpected events and to find time for studying as well as for work and extracurricular activities. Many students report that study tasks take longer than planned, leading to the feeling that they are getting nowhere. Many students also report that they find that they cannot keep up with regular study tasks because they need to work to immediate deadlines. However hard they work, they feel as though there are a million other things still to be done.

SELF-ASSESSMENT OF CURRENT APPROACH TO TIME MANAGEMENT

Read over the following statements, and think about how each one matches your experience with time management. Score each statement from 1 (this is not typical of me) up to 5 (this is very typical of me).

_____ 1. I make sure that I know the dates for my tests and due dates for assignments.

_____ 2. I use a calendar or wall planner to display key dates.

_____ 3. I keep my day planner up to date and look at it daily.

_____ 4. I list key tasks to be done each day.

_____ 5. I prioritize tasks to be done each week.

_____ 6. I know which times of day work best for me as study times.

_____ 7. I am able to resist pressure from friends if I have work to do.

_____ 8. I get started quickly when I sit down to study.

_____ 9. I work where I can concentrate and won't be disturbed.

_____ 10. I make sure to accomplish some studying every day.

_____ 11. I set a high priority on my own effective time management.

_____ 12. I plan for recreation/relaxation time each week.

_____ 13. I begin to work on assignments well ahead of the due date.

_____ 14. I am well prepared for tests.

_____ 15. I reward myself when I have completed my priority tasks.

My Total Score _____

EVALUATING YOUR RESPONSES

Each of the above statements is a sound time-management strategy. As there are 15 statements in this list, each ranked from 1–5, your total score can range anywhere from a low of 15 to a high of 75. If you score at the low end of this range—say, below 30—then you need to work on your time-management strategies. If you score at the high end—say, above 60—then you have established a sound approach to your own time management and may be ready to adopt more effective learning strategies.

A STEP-BY-STEP TIME-MANAGEMENT SYSTEM

By following the five steps to effective time management, you can take control of time and make it work to your advantage.

- 1: Identify Your Difficulties with Time Management
- 2: Make a Careful Assessment of Your Current Activities
- 3: Plan Ahead and Keep a Schedule
- 4: Make the Most of Each Study Session
- 5: Evaluate Your Time-Management Plan Regularly

1: IDENTIFY YOUR DIFFICULTIES WITH TIME MANAGEMENT

Before you can implement an effective personal time-management system, you have to recognize that you need to take action. Begin by being very honest with yourself in your assessment of how successful you are at managing your time. What system do you use? Does it work for you? If your answer is *"Yes, my system does work for me,"* then what do you see as the strengths of your system? If your answer is *"No, I am not a good time planner,"* what are the problems as you see them?

1. How do you currently manage your time?

   _____

   _____

2. What works well with your current system?

   _____

   _____

3. What does not work well with your current system?

   _____

   _____

4. How motivated are you to learn about and apply time-management strategies? Rank yourself on a scale of 1 (not motivated) to 10 (highly motivated).

   1   2   3   4   5   6   7   8   9   10

You are the one in charge, and you have to make the decision to manage your time and to follow through on your plans. If you feel motivated at this point to give a systematic time-management plan a try, continue with the following steps to effective personal time management.

2: Make a Careful Assessment of Your Current Activities

Use Table 3.1 to gather information on your activities. In your mind, go over a couple of typical days and try not to miss any essential activities. For example, students sometimes forget to include travel time, which can be significant! Then complete the table, using the following checklist as a guide.

- ☑ List all the activities that you must, or would like to, find time for.
- ☑ Estimate how much time (hours per week) each activity will require.
- ☑ Note which activities will take place regularly or occasionally.
- ☑ Label each activity as either essential or optional.
- ☑ Rank each activity on a scale of high/medium/low priority.

When you have completed the table, look over the activities and give yourself time to digest the information that you have gathered. You may find that you have listed more activities than you have time for. What activities are least important? What choices do you have? Can you decide on your priorities?

Your most important choices have to do with your academic program (for example, the course load you wish to take). In some programs, you have to take a full load of courses. For example, if you are aiming for an honours or limited-enrolment program, or if you want to play on a school sports team, there may be mandatory academic requirements that you have to meet. If you want to do volunteer work or are paying for your education by working at a part-time job that takes more than 15 hours per week you may have to consider reducing your course load, as it is easy to fall behind with necessary school work and then find tests and assignments to be intimidating and stressful. If you overload your academic activities, you may find that you lose energy because you are not taking time to recharge your batteries.

In addition, if you are committed to working or volunteering for more than 15 hours a week then you may also miss the critical social and recreational benefits of being a student. Good choices are essential to reaching your academic potential, and you are in charge of those choices.

TABLE 3.1   Assessment of Current Activities

ACTIVITIES	HOURS PER WEEK	REGULAR OR OCCASIONAL	ESSENTIAL OR OPTIONAL	PRIORITY: HIGH/ MEDIUM/ LOW

3: PLAN AHEAD AND KEEP A SCHEDULE

Most sudents who are really successful plan ahead for key events. When you record the dates of tests, assignments, and other personal commitments, you are more likely to follow through and do the necessary work. Design a weekly timetable and a term-long calendar—either on paper or on your computer or hand-held organizer.

☑ Plan for the term and mark important assignment and test dates on a wall calendar. As soon as you get your course outlines, review them for significant dates and deadlines and enter these in your planner. Also, listen in class for additional information that may not have been available in the course outline, and add any new dates to your planner.

☑ Add dates for important nonacademic activities, and try to maintain a balance with your academic activities. You need to monitor the amount of time you are spending on activities such as committees, fitness and recreation activities, or at a part-time job. If you plan far enough in advance, you can make adjustments so they do not interfere with high-priority academic commitments. Such preparation requires self-discipline, and it may be helpful to plan joint study sessions that enforce planning and thinking ahead.

☑ Post a weekly timetable in a prominent location with all of your regular class times marked. Indicate (maybe in red) some blocks of time that you are going to reserve on a regular basis for out-of-class study. If you can develop a regular study timetable, you will find that your work gets completed and that you feel in control of all of your work.

☑ Use a day planner or other system to plan a tentative schedule of study tasks that you wish to accomplish in a week. You may not always follow the schedule rigidly, but it will guide your daily planning. Keep in mind two key strategies: (a) using your best times of day to study, and (b) using small blocks of time between other activities. Look at the sample of a weekly timetable that was created by a student (Table 3.2). Then use the blank weekly timetable (Table 3.3) to plan a week of studying.

☑ Each evening, think about what you want to get done the next day, and record your study tasks for that day. Collect all necessary notes and texts that you will need to follow through on your plans.

4: MAKE THE MOST OF EACH STUDY SESSION

When you sit down to study, establish your priorities and set realistic study goals. You want to maximize your level of concentration so that you move along with the study task as efficiently as possible. You will get a great sense of achievement if you optimize each work session in this way.

☑ Review your time schedule and identify priority tasks.

☑ Estimate how long you will spend on each task.

☑ Work to achieve each study goal you have set.

☑ Take small, appropriate breaks to keep your energy and concentration levels high.

☑ Check off the tasks in your daily planner as you complete them.

TABLE 3.2   Completed Weekly Timetable

	Monday	Tuesday	Wednesday	Thursday	Friday	Saturday	Sunday
7:00–8:00	←		Breakfast		→		
8:00–9:00		↑		Math Tutorial	↑ Geog Lab		
9:00–10:00		Bio Lab	↑				
10:00–11:00		↓	Chem Lab				
11:00–12:00	Swim	Geog 020	↓	Geog 020	Lunch		
12:00–1:00	Math 027	Lunch	Math 027	Lunch	Math 027		
1:00–2:00	Lunch	Physics 020	Lunch	Physics 020			
2:00–3:00	Chem 020		Chem 020	↑			
3:00–4:00	↑ Bio 020		Squash	Physics Lab			
4:00–5:00	↓	Swim	Swim	↓	Swim		
5:00–6:00	←		Dinner		→		
6:00–7:00				↑			
7:00–8:00				Squash Club			
8:00–9:00				↓			
9:00–10:00							
10:00–11:00							

☐ Planned Study Time   ⬚ Flexible Study Time

TABLE 3.3   Blank Weekly Timetable

	Monday	Tuesday	Wednesday	Thursday	Friday	Saturday	Sunday
7:00–8:00							
8:00–9:00							
9:00–10:00							
10:00–11:00							
11:00–12:00							
12:00–1:00							
1:00–2:00							
2:00–3:00							
3:00–4:00							
4:00–5:00							
5:00–6:00							
6:00–7:00							
7:00–8:00							
8:00–9:00							
9:00–10:00							
10:00–11:00							

5: EVALUATE YOUR TIME-MANAGEMENT PLAN REGULARLY

Take time at least once a week to review your progress. If you are not meeting your study goals, what are the reasons? If it is because you did not follow through with your study plans, you may need to remind yourself of your academic goals and your motivation to do well. Think about how you can be more successful at meeting your goals in the coming week, and reset some manageable goals. Are you spending several hours at a desk but still wasting a good chunk of that time in daydreaming or worrying? If this is a common problem for you, then read the next section on procrastination and also Chapter 9, "Managing the Stress of Being a Student," very carefully. If you were putting in a real effort but just couldn't meet your goals, try the following:

☑ Prioritize your most important tasks and reschedule those that need more time to complete.

☑ Adjust your tentative schedule for the remainder of the week.

☑ Think creatively about how you are completing tasks. Can you think of any timesavers?

☑ If you continually experience real time-management problems, monitor your activities carefully and decide if you can make constructive adjustments by yourself. If you are not satisfied with how things are going, seek help from your instructor or learning skills counsellor.

RECORDING AND ANALYZING TIME SPENT

If you are having difficulties with time management, monitor your time for three typical weekdays. Use Table 3.4 to record your activities hour by hour. Pay particular attention to out-of-class study time. Use this information to find out how much time you are spending on different activities by completing Table 3.5. You may be able to adjust your planning based on this information. It will also be a useful starting point for getting help from your instructor or counsellor.

TABLE 3.4   Blank Timetable for Analyzing Time Spent

	Monday	Tuesday	Wednesday	Thursday	Friday
7:00					
8:00					
9:00					
10:00					
11:00					
12:00					
1:00					
2:00					
3:00					
4:00					
5:00					
6:00					
7:00					
8:00					
9:00					
10:00					
11:00					

TABLE 3.5   Analysis of Three Study Days

ACTIVITIES	HOURS			
	DAY 1	DAY 2	DAY 3	TOTAL
Class				
Study				
Travel				
Exercise				
Meals and Chores				
Leisure				
Sleep				
TOTAL				

1. Fill in the total hours of study time for each course. List the tasks that were done.

COURSE	HOURS	TASKS
1.		
2.		
3.		
4.		
5.		

2. Can you see which times of the day are good for

serious concentration?

less-demanding study tasks?

3. Can you detect a time that is not productive for studying?

STRATEGIES TO MAINTAIN AND ENHANCE YOUR SYSTEM

Once you have established a time-management system, consider how the following additional strategies can help you maintain momentum and adapt to additional needs:

- Make Each Day Count by Using Small Blocks of Time
- Know and Use Your Best Times for Concentration
- Plan for Meals and Recreation
- Plan Adequate Study Time for Courses You Dislike
- Review Your Lecture Notes Soon after the Class
- Spread Out Learning of Memory Material

MAKE EACH DAY COUNT BY USING SMALL BLOCKS OF TIME

Aim to get some high-priority tasks completed each day. You can do a good deal of important work in an hour or less: reviewing class notes, reading part of a chapter, doing a few math problems, going to see an instructor.

KNOW AND USE YOUR BEST TIMES FOR CONCENTRATION

When are your best times for concentration? It is likely that there are certain times in each day when you are more able to do tasks that require careful attention. In contrast, there may be other times of the day when it is more difficult for you to study efficiently. Most people are more alert during daytime hours. Whenever possible, try to use your peak times for studying rather than for less challenging activities.

PLAN FOR MEALS AND RECREATION

Your studying is of prime importance, but it is equally important to look after other personal needs. A healthy lifestyle is crucial to your enjoyment of student life and your ability to study effectively. Make time for nutritious meals, regular exercise, and a reasonable amount of relaxation. Your progress will suffer if you shortchange your health, especially during exams when it is even more crucial that you get exercise, eat well, and get enough sleep, because you are under more stress and require extra energy.

PLAN ADEQUATE STUDY TIME FOR COURSES YOU DISLIKE

Many students make the mistake of studying long hours on courses they like and putting little time into courses they dislike. You need to plan to spend adequate time across all your study tasks and may need to organize some reward for completing those in your less favourite courses. Another strategy is to join a group of students so that you can keep up with assigned tasks, exchange information about course concepts, and collaborate on review sessions for tests.

REVIEW YOUR LECTURE NOTES SOON AFTER THE CLASS

Brief, same-day review of lecture notes can be a very powerful time-saving strategy, especially if your notes are not as complete or organized as they might be. Typing your handwritten notes into your computer might help you to clarify the ideas, but limit this approach to class notes that are not in good shape. By doing some kind of active but brief review of your lecture notes on or near the day of the lecture, you can save many hours of "relearning." (See Chapter 4, "Learning from Lectures," for more details.)

SPREAD OUT LEARNING OF MEMORY MATERIAL

In courses where you need to memorize detailed information, such as biology, psychology, or economics, three one-hour study periods throughout the week will be more effective for you than a single three-hour chunk. Your memory needs time to process new information and ideas, so it is much more efficient to distribute this kind of study in smaller chunks across your schedule.[1]

PROCRASTINATION

Understanding procrastination is not easy, because it is a complex behaviour that can be both the cause and the result of academic stress. Just about every student procrastinates at some time for a variety of reasons.

SYMPTOMS OF PROCRASTINATION

- **Feelings of inertia:** You do not feel like doing anything, especially school work, even if it is critical that you do it. It takes less energy to continue with the same activity—especially if it is having a cup of coffee or watching TV—than to find the energy to begin something new.
- **Preoccupation with "loose ends" or minor tasks:** You feel it is important to finish one thing completely and perfectly before going on to another. This approach can mean that you ignore more important tasks until it is too late to do a good job.

- **Being swamped with work:** With many things to do, all claiming equal priority, you can find it hard to decide where to begin. You may get overwhelmed and take the line of least resistance by not getting started on anything.
- **Confusion:** You may be confused about the nature and scope of an assigment. For example, you do not know how to identify the thesis statement or incorporate reference material in your research paper. It's easier to put it aside than to try to figure it out.
- **Overinvolvement in other activities:** Other activities (e.g., sports, socializing, movies) seem to have more payoff than studying, especially in the short term.
- **Seeking the company of others:** Like many tasks, studying is isolating. Most of the time, it has to be done alone. If you are feeling lonely and looking for an excuse not to work, you may go looking for someone to talk to instead of getting down to work.
- **Feelings of guilt:** What is being neglected for study? Other things require your time and attention—your friends, family, church, the dog. Taking time to study may seem to be taking time away from others. Guilt feelings interfere with your attention, and you get nothing done.

UNDERSTANDING PROCRASTINATION

Have you noticed that you can often find activities other than studying that appear to be worthwhile: spending time at the gym (it's good to be fit), participating in club activities (great experience on the résumé), and volunteering (valuable career exploration)? However, these useful activities can all be substitutes for studying. If you feel that you procrastinate regularly, then you need to ask yourself some questions. *"What function does procrastination play?" "Why do I want to avoid studying?"* Three explanations for procrastination that you might consider are:

- Fear of Failure
- Fear of Success
- Avoidance of Control

FEAR OF FAILURE

You may have doubts about whether you can be successful in a course. If you set yourself very high standards then you may be afraid that whatever you do will not be good enough. Many students find that their need to get high grades and to produce perfect assignments creates serious pressure for them. By procrastinating, you give yourself an excuse for not performing well by putting in too little time to do the necessary work. If you were to work hard but not get a good grade, then you might have to consider that you do not have the necessary skill or ability—a much more difficult realization than attributing a poor grade to lack of effort.[2]

FEAR OF SUCCESS

Have you considered that your commitment to study may be influenced by anticipation of unpleasant consequences from doing well? For example, either consciously or unconsciously, you may fear that your relationship with classmates will suffer or that your parents, your partner, or the instructor may expect even higher standards of performance in the future. Such increased pressure can affect your personal expectations and cause your stress level to rise. Consequently, you may decide that life will be simpler if you put less effort into studying. The negative and discouraging result is that you will not reach your peak potential performance level.

AVOIDANCE OF CONTROL

Perhaps you feel too controlled by others—the school rules, instructors or parents who expect you to meet the educational challenge. You may feel that you want to establish your own independent identity rather than do what is more predictable. In the short term, not making an effort to study appears to be a way of taking control and "rebelling." If you are unsure about your choice of program or you feel that you were pressured to achieve in elementary or high school, avoidance may appeal to you as a good way to escape.

YOU AND PROCRASTINATION

What are the symptoms of procrastination that you display?

_____

_____

_____

Can you give any reasons for the times when you did procrastinate?

_____

_____

_____

REMEDIES FOR PROCRASTINATION

If you are to overcome procrastination, you need to take some small and realistic steps to getting your time management back on track. Keep in mind the five steps of time management that you have read about in this chapter, and as you work at putting a plan into place apply the following remedies for procrastination.

☑ Substitute the mental message "I should" with" "I'd like to."

☑ Set up a reward for finishing something so that you are more likely to take the initiative.

☑ Begin your study session with a study task that is not too demanding.

☑ Subdivide a bigger task into several smaller chunks, say, 15-minute items. This can reduce the level of difficulty of the overall task.

☑ Suspend your criticism about how well you are doing long enough to complete a task for the first time.

☑ Cooperate with a friend to share a task and to reduce isolation.

What strategies do you intend to use to make sure that procrastination does not have a negative effect on your academic performance?

_____

_____

_____

_____

WHAT ARE YOUR SUGGESTIONS FOR TIME MANAGEMENT?

If you were asked to help students with their time-management issues, what strategies would you suggest? In this exercise on time management, suggested strategies for Maria have been provided as a model. Complete the exercise by writing down three learning strategies for each of the problems that Andrew, Kirsten, and Daniel have presented to you.

Maria has been spending more and more of her time talking with her friends than preparing for class. She knows that she has problems managing her time and wants to do something about it. What time-management strategies can you suggest to Maria to get her started in the right direction?

1. <u>Maria can make an assessment of the previous two days so that she has a clearer idea of how she is using or wasting her time.</u>

2. <u>She can make a list of the most important tasks she has to accomplish and prioritize them.</u>

3. <u>She can plan a time and place for that evening when she will work on her highest-priority task.</u>

Andrew is a first-year student who is taking a full load of courses. Money is very tight for him and he has been offered a part-time job that would really help out with the finances. How can he maintain his grades in his courses as well as work 15 hours a week at this job?

1. _____

_____

2. _____

_____

3. _____

_____

Kirsten has come to university to meet new people and expand her horizons. Her studies are important to her, but she also wants to have an active social life. How can she make the most of each day so that both her studies and social life are not neglected?

1. _____

_____

2. _____

_____

3. _____

_____

Daniel is in a typical first-year program and has lots of school work to do. He has told everyone that he wants to get into medical school but he is very worried about getting the necessary grades, and so tends to put things off. He knows that he is a procrastinator and wants to make a new start. What are three remedies for procrastination that he could try?

1. _____

_____

2. _____

_____

3. _____

_____

SUCCESSFUL TIME MANAGEMENT

The two major challenges that you face in managing your time will be to find the right balance between your academic and nonacademic activities and to apply yourself consistently to those activities that lead to success. If you can meet these challenges, your years in school will be very rewarding as you grow both academically and socially as part of a broader community. Time-management skills that you develop and that work for you as a student will stay with you and enhance your later career and personal life.

This chapter stressed self-management of time and led you through a five-step process that included exploring your motivation; assessing your current activities; and planning, implementing, and evaluating your time-management system. You can maintain the system and add flexibility by regularly applying additional general strategies of time management. The chapter also addressed how you can understand and overcome your tendency to procrastinate. Your time-management system can be further enhanced if you develop strategies to improve your concentration. These are addressed in Chapter 9, "Managing the Stress of Being a Student."

 **WEB ALERT!**

Mount Royal College
Calgary, Alberta
www.mtroyal.ab.ca/studentlife/study_time.shtml
Student Life: Studying and Writing Effectively—Managing Time

York University—Glendon
Toronto, Ontario
www.yorku.ca/gcareers/time_management.htm
Time Management. This is a list of suggested links to sites with excellent time-management information.

Lethbridge College
Lethbridge, Alberta
www.lethbridgecollege.ab.ca/departments/student/learning/quicktip/procrast.html
Quick Tips: Procrastination

CHAPTER ENDNOTES

1. Bransford, J., Brown, A., & Cocking, R. (1999). *How people learn: Brain, mind, experience and school.* Washington, DC: National Academy Press.
2. Burka, J. B., & Yuen, L. M. (1983). *Procrastination: Why you do it, what to do about it.* New York: HarperCollins.

Chapter 4

LEARNING FROM LECTURES

LEARNING OBJECTIVES

The purpose of this chapter is for you to:
• Think about your role in lectures.
• Develop a strategic approach to listening in class.
• Learn effective strategies for lecture note taking.
• Evaluate effective review strategies for lecture notes.
• Think about appropriate abbreviations and graphic organizers for your notes.
• Assess how to handle problem lectures.

When you start a course, one of your first challenges is to learn how to take complete and well-organized notes as you listen for, select, and record key information. In this chapter, you will think about your general strategies for learning from lectures. This may happen in a fairly small class in which you can readily ask questions of your instructor, or it might be in a much larger class of more than 1,000 students, for example. In a very large class, you will have less direct contact with your instructor but probably more contact with teaching assistants who are there to help you. Whatever your learning style, strengths, or weaknesses, and whatever the format of the class, you need to come to grips with lectures and consider how you can make your learning in lectures as effective as possible. Many of the strategies for note taking in this chapter emphasize ideas of organization and structure in information. You will find more on this topic in Chapter 6, "Effective Memory."

SELF-ASSESSMENT OF CURRENT APPROACH TO LECTURES

Read over the following statements, and think about classes you have attended in the past. How do these statements match your experience? Score each statement from 1 (this is not typical of me) up to 5 (this is very typical of me).

1. I attend every lecture.
2. I prepare for the lecture by completing required readings before going to class.
3. I check the course outline regularly to keep track of topics covered in the course.
4. I go into each class determined to learn as much as possible.
5. I sit where I can see and hear easily.
6. I concentrate on the teacher and try to ignore distractions going on around me.
7. In class I work hard to control any worry thoughts or daydreaming.
8. I summarize just the main points of the lecture, rather than write down every word.
9. I echo in my mind what has just been said, so that I can record that point while listening to the next.
10. If I lose track of what the teacher is saying, I don't give up and I try to reconnect with the topic.
11. I listen for connections among ideas and emphasize that structure in my notes.

_____   12. I take notes that are easy to read and meaningful.

_____   13. If I don't understand something in class, I get help as soon as possible.

_____   14. Within a few hours of the class, I read over the notes I have taken.

_____   15. When I go over my notes after class, I make the headings stand out by underlining or highlighting them.

_____

My Total Score _____

EVALUATING YOUR RESPONSES

Each of the above statements is a sound strategy that can help you learn effectively from lectures. As there are 15 statements in this list, each ranked from 1–5, your total score can range anywhere from a low of 15 to a high of 75. If you score at the low end of this range—say, below 30—then you need to work on your strategies for learning from lectures. If you score at the high end—say, above 60—then you have already established a sound approach to lectures.

YOUR ROLE IN THE LECTURE

IDENTIFY THE PURPOSE OF THE LECTURE

You need to evaluate how the lecture fits with other components of the course, so you can take the most appropriate approach to note taking. Here are some lecture options: the instructor introduces completely new information that is not in your text; the lecture is used to review and expand upon required readings; the lecture is a time for discussion among students in the class either based on required readings or on case studies you have prepared. Your approach will vary with each type of lecture. You will need excellent note-taking skills to get a record of new material, while you may be able to spend more time listening and discussing if you are adequately prepared for a class based on readings or cases.

BE PREPARED FOR VARIED DELIVERY OF CONTENT

The word *lecture* comes from a Latin word meaning "to read," and you may have classes with a teacher simply reading prepared notes to you. However, with audiovisual aids and computers in the classroom, you are much more likely to find yourself in a class where the content is delivered in a variety of ways. You will be looking at prepared overheads or computer-based presentations while your instructor talks about the diagram or limited amount of text projected on the screen. You may also find yourself watching a segment of film or some slides. Whatever the delivery or light level in the room, you need to get down an adequate record of the information.

Use Course Resources Appropriately

Your instructor will provide you with a detailed course outline, which will usually list the support resources available to you. Many instructors provide lecture outlines or more detailed notes, either through the class website or sometimes sold as a course package through the campus bookstore. If notes are provided for you, make sure to use them appropriately. For example, they may only be a bare-bones outline, and you will need to fill in all of the extra details as you listen to the class so that you are not missing essential details when you use those notes for review for tests.

Try to Do as Much Learning during Lectures as Possible

Go into class with a keen interest in both learning as much as possible and recording notes in a meaningful way. As obvious as this seems, a careful look at the behaviour of many students in lectures indicates something different. Some students talk to friends, read the newspaper, or stare off into space. Also, some students suffer from "stenographer's syndrome"—trying to write down every word rather than being selective.

Monitor Your Comprehension

As you listen to the lecture, evaluate whether you understand the ideas. If you find the lecture content difficult, you need to get back to your notes as soon as possible after class, and you may need to check things out with your instructor or teaching assistant. See Chapter 6, "Effective Memory," for a list of symptoms of comprehension problems.

Work on Developing Your Learning Strategies for Lectures

Many of the strategies presented in this chapter do not come naturally—you need to develop them. Depending on your learning style, some strategies will be easy for you to adopt—listening for the auditory learner, recording for the visual learner, and participating in discussion and presentations for the tactile/kinesthetic learner—while others will be more of a challenge. Whatever your preferred learning style, all aspects of learning from lectures are key activities, and necessary to effective learning. As you read through the strategies for listening, recording, and reviewing class notes, put a checkmark by any strategy that you do *not* currently use, and when you have finished the chapter look back at the strategies you have checked and make decisions about which new strategies you will practise when you go to your next lecture. The next few pages demonstrate one sound strategy: putting key words in the margin.[1] This should be done soon after class to consolidate information in your long-term memory.

Listening

– Be an active listener

LISTENING STRATEGIES

Active listening will help you to get as much as possible from a lecture. Try the following:

Prepare before class

– Read before class
– Check course outline
– Maintain energy

– Intend to learn
– Sit in good spot
– Aim for continuity

Before the Lecture

- Survey or read the required readings before class so that you can more readily recognize new ideas and vocabulary.
- Check your course outline to keep track of the sequence of topics.
- Go to class with enough physical and mental energy to stay alert for the whole time period. If you go to class tired, it will be difficult to concentrate.
- Go to class intending to learn as much as you can.

- Sit where you can keep your attention on the instructor and see and hear as well as possible.
- As the class is settling down, quickly look over your notes from the previous class. This will help you with continuity of topics.

In class

– Listen for outline
– Watch for clues

During the Lecture

- Listen for opening statements outlining topics, format, or philosophy.
- Watch and listen to your instructor and not the rest of the class. Pay particular attention to emphasis of major points through voice modulations, pauses, body movements, and so on. These cues will help you to discriminate between main ideas and supporting information.

– Identify
  structure

– Link old
  with new

– Ask questions

– Stay alert

- Look for organization in the class content. If the lecture is not well structured, try to organize your notes under headings and subheadings that you identify for yourself.
- To make the lecture as meaningful as possible, try to connect the new information you are hearing in class with what you already know.
- If you do not understand a point, ask your instructor to go over it again. You can do this either in class or after class during your instructor's office hours.
- Be aware that by the middle of the lecture your attention may lapse. Take a few deep breaths, sit up straight and stretch your back, and direct your attention back to the class.

RECORDING STRATEGIES

Recording

– Develop a
  good system
– Structure,
  structure,
  structure

Consider taking class lecture notes on loose-leaf paper that you can store in a ring binder. This tends to be a better system than a notebook, as you can file handouts with the relevant lecture. In the lecture, focus on making your notes as organized and meaningful as possible. Pay particular attention to the way in which the material is structured under subheadings. You will learn more in the lecture and have less to do on your own afterward, and your notes will be much easier to read, edit, and review after class.

Overall system

– Number
  pages
– Write on one
  side of paper

– Add mar-
  ginal notes
  for review
– Leave white
  space

Overall Organization of Notes

- Make sure that pages are dated or numbered in some way, so you can easily keep them in the correct order.
- Write on only one side of the paper. You can then use the other side of the page to add information from the text, your own examples, questions you need to ask the instructor, or review questions.
- Draw a 2-inch (5 cm) margin down one side of each page, and when you review your notes after class use this margin to add key words to highlight main ideas.
- Leave white space on the page so you can add comments later. Also, your notes will look better and be easier to review for a test.

Ways to Organize Information in Notes

Organize
content
- Identify big
  picture

- Listen for
  outline

- Make head-
  ings stand out
- Use indents

- Use lists
- Draw clear
  diagrams

- Vary layout

- Even if your instructor does not give the lecture a title, come up with one for each class by asking yourself the question, *"What is this all about?"*
- If your instructor presents an outline at the beginning of the class, copy it down and use it to track the sequence of topics as you structure your notes.
- Highlight headings and subheadings so the organizing ideas stand out from the details.
- Indent related information under each subheading. This emphasis on structure will enhance your long-term memory of the information.
- Identify lists of important details with bullets, numbers, or letters.
- Make graphs and diagrams easy to read and label them well, so they are meaningful to you later on. Visual aids, such as diagrams, are critical to long-term memory.
- Vary your layout to suit the content. As many lectures present a lot of information relatively quickly, for most of your classes you will likely use point form or short paragraphs to record this flow of ideas. For certain types of information, however, you may be able to organize your notes in a more graphic form to highlight relationships (see p. 59 for more on graphic organizers).

REVIEW STRATEGIES FOR LECTURE NOTES

Review
- Review
  strengthens
  LTM

Review your notes soon after class to reinforce that information in your long-term memory. If you also review your class notes occasionally during the term, this will take a lot of pressure off when you are getting ready for a test.

Review Strategies

After class

- Review soon
  after class
- Check structure

- Find a regular time (15–20 minutes) within 24 hours of the lecture to go over the notes that you took in class.
- Check that the organization and structure of ideas stand out.

– Add marginal key words

– Make up review questions

– Identify problems

– Include my own comments

– Share ideas

– Plan periodic review

NOTE: Recopying not effective

- Add key words to the margin to summarize main points. Note that this chapter demonstrates this strategy.
- Make up two or three review questions for each lecture. You will be anticipating possible test questions.
- If you are unclear on any points in the lecture, write down questions to ask your instructor or another student in the class, and then go back and rewrite this point in your notes.
- Add any personal reflections or expansion on the topic on the blank page or in white space in your notes.
- Talk with friends about the ideas presented in class.
- Reread key words every few weeks to refresh your memory of the lectures.
- Avoid simple recopying of your notes! It uses up a lot of study time, and you do not learn much because you are not actively selecting and organizing information. The only exception would be if you come out of class knowing that your notes are disorganized, incomplete, or unclear.

USING ABBREVIATIONS

Many lectures in college and university move so quickly that it seems impossible to get everything down. Worse yet, instructors may write nothing down as they talk, but you are still expected to record notes. How can you handle this situation? You need strategies for abbreviating information as you write, with the goal of capturing the meaning of each important idea in a brief, yet accurate manner. Not only do abbreviations allow you to get down much more information, they also force you to focus on the meaning of the material and not simply on the words or letters. You can abbreviate your notes in the following ways:

- Use symbols, especially for identifying relationships.
- Abbreviate words that you use frequently.
- Shorten complex sentences by leaving out less important words. Make sure to leave enough of the sentence so that you can reconstruct the full meaning when you study from your notes, especially after several weeks have passed since you took them.

If, when you review your notes after the class, you think that you have over-abbreviated the content, expand your notes again so that they are more meaningful over the long term.

Useful Symbols for Relationships

∴ therefore, thus, or so
∵ because, since
↑ increase
↓ decrease
= equal to, same as
χ psychology

∝ is related to, depends on
→ leads to, implies that
& or + and, in addition to
vs versus; cf compare/contrast
< less than; > greater than
~ about, approximately

Examples of Abbreviations for Commonly Used Words

def^n = definition
eg = example
evid = evidence
inp = input
fxn = function
ind = individual
tech = technique
av = average
bkgd = background
gov't = government
bhvr = behaviour

mech = mechanism
ps = problem solving
soc = sociology
psych = psychology
w = with
observ = observation
inf = information
$comp^n$ = composition
enuf = enough
imp = important
Cdn = Canadian

An Example of Leaving Out Words

The original statement:

> Examples like these lead researchers to hypothesize that successful problem-solving behaviour depends more on the structure of the knowledge base rather than on the content of that knowledge base.

Abbreviated note:

> Researchers hypothesize that successful problem solvers depend more on structure of knowledge base than on content.

Your Abbreviations

Abbreviate the paragraph below, using all three methods for abbreviating—symbols, abbreviating words, and leaving out less important words. In addition to any abbreviations that you use from the above lists, generate your own if you feel they are appropriate; there are no right or wrong ways to abbreviate—just whatever works for you. Check when you have finished that your abbreviations don't affect your understanding of the content.

> Psychologists use systematic techniques to observe and describe behaviour. In *naturalistic observation,* the researcher observes behaviour in natural settings rather than in a laboratory environment. Naturalistic observation is a useful technique for generating research ideas and for verifying whether conclusions reached in the lab generalize to more realistic settings. In *case studies,* the focus is on a single example of a behaviour or psychological phenomenon. This technique allows the researcher to obtain lots of background information on the individual being studied, but the results may not always generalize to wider populations. In *survey research,* behaviour is surveyed broadly, usually by gathering questionnaire responses from many people. Finally through *psychological tests,* differences between individuals can be quantified.[2]

_____

_____

_____

_____

_____

_____

GRAPHIC ORGANIZERS

You will already be familiar with graphic (visual) organizers, as instructors commonly use them as teaching aids. What would a geography class be without a map, or a psychology class without a table that places key information into a set of categories? Graphic organizers are simply-drawn frameworks of lines and/or curves that you can use as aids to organizing information, and they do not have to be complex to be effective. Perhaps the simplest is a box drawn around some key information in your notes. Each time you look over that page, the box will immediately re-focus your attention on that important item.

As many lectures move quite quickly and can present a lot of information, it is best in class to use fairly simple shapes as graphic organizers. As you get used to the content of each course, you can select a few shapes to use on a regular basis. These will help you to identify that all-important structure in the information. After class, when you review your notes and are better able to see the big picture of the lecture, you might create more complex graphic organizers to summarize some key ideas. They will add visual impact to your notes, making them easier to review for tests.

Figure 4.1, "Page and Graphic Organizers," illustrates three alternatives for subdividing your note pages in class, and it highlights a variety of graphic organizers to use in class or when reviewing notes after class. You will also find two examples of graphic organizers, used to summarize novels, in Chapter 8, "Focus on the Social Sciences and Humanities."

EXAMPLES OF STRATEGIC NOTE TAKING

Figures 4.2 and 4.3 are sample pages of notes taken by first-year students who are both Good Strategy Users: Figure 4.2 is from a political science lecture in which the instructor used a lot of overheads to illustrate points about class-consciousness; Figure 4.3 is from an earth sciences lecture in which the instructor showed a short film to illustrate a natural system of earth movements. So how did these Good Strategy Users end up with good notes and sound knowledge of this material? Here are the note-taking strategies they used:

BEFORE THE LECTURE

1. They checked their course outlines to see which topics were being covered in class, so they both knew what to expect.
2. They thought about the kinds of relationships that would be stressed in these lectures. The political science student realized that his lecture would basically be an academic argument presenting competing viewpoints on class-consciousness in Canada.[3] The earth sciences student recognized that her lecture would cover a natural system occurring in the real world. She realized that the focus would be on comparing different types of volcanoes, with an emphasis on mechanisms producing the different types.
3. The students prepared notepaper they would be using in class by drawing a 2-inch (5 cm) margin down one side, so that marginal summary notes could be added later when they reviewed their notes after class.

DURING THE LECTURE

1. They paid close attention in class.
2. They dated and numbered lecture pages
3. They used abbreviations.

FIGURE 4.1   Page and Graphic Organizers

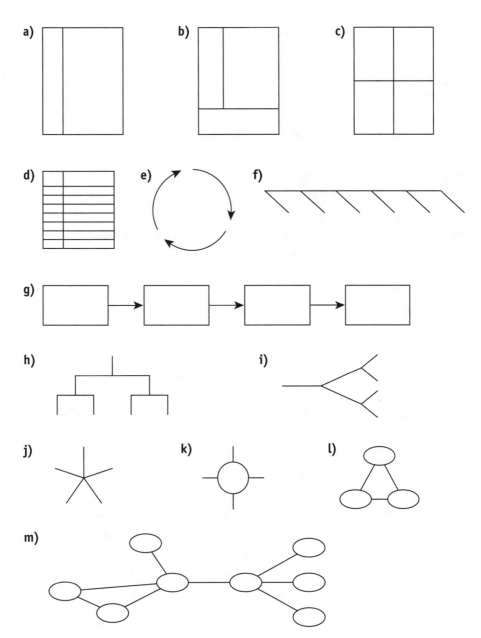

Different ways to organize pages for in-class note-taking are shown in a), b), and c). Note that style b), with a margin for key words down the left side and a space at the bottom for your reflections, is the Cornell method for notes. Graphic organizers are d) table; e) cycle; f) timeline; g) flowchart; h) and i) trees: hierarchical; j), k), and l) simple webs; and m) complex web.

FIGURE 4.2   A Sample Page of Political Science Lecture Notes

	Political Science 020 Feb 14. p. 1
key question to explore: poor/Canada/class-consciousness	<u>Class-consciousness in Canada</u> Why do the poor in Canada lack a sense of their class even as social programs decline?
<u>one side of the argument</u>	<u>Argument #1</u> Those happy with system
soc'y grouped on other criteria social mobility happens	• divisions other than class more evident in society and have more social influence • social mobility common in Canada • most of the pop'n feels middle class • material benefits are shared by all
<u>counter argument</u>	<u>Argument #2</u> NOT happy with system
upper/middle classes rule the roost! poor powerless	• upper/middle classes define political relevance • differences based on region, ethnicity, and religion • who is friend or foe is based on the above (reg/eth/rel) • unions don't pull together – divisive • the poor don't have resources to challenge the status quo • those in power see differences as result of individual effort – not class

4. They took notes, using headings, indenting, white space, and bullets. The earth sciences student made notes even though the light level in class was low.

5. They looked for structure in the content and used a layout to best fit that structure.

FIGURE 4.3   A Sample Page of Earth Sciences Lecture Notes

Earth Sciences 100   Nov 6.   p. 1

Type of Volcanoes (film)

Type of Volcanoes Strato

1. <u>Strato volcanoes</u> — composite/layered, High, large
   eg. Mt. Fuji, Mt. St. Helens
   Canad. egs in BC ancient (extinct?) weathered down

Subduction zones
*** assoc. with sub-duction zones
- very dangerous, explosive, occasional eruptions

Explosive – viscous
- Viscous lava, moves slowly
- Results from many explosions (lava, rock debris, etc)
- Av. comp^n andesite

Shield

2. <u>Shield volcanoes</u> – flatish, very extensive
   eg. Mauna Loa, Hawaii; Iceland
   Canad. eg. Mt. Edziza in BC

Hot spots
*** at hot spots in the crust
- Very fluid magma – easy flow

very fluid – frequent
- Results from many eruptions (can be thin layers)
- basaltic

Scoria

3. <u>Scoria volcanoes</u> cinder cones – small, steep sided
   Common on strato & shield volcanoes
   Canad. eg. On Mt. Edziza in BC

Vents on strato or shield
*** around vents on strato or shield volc.

Cinder/ash – single event
- Cinder and ash – solidified gas bubbles
- Usually one-time event
- basaltic

AFTER THE LECTURE

1. They each spent 15 minutes after class actively reviewing the notes they had taken in class and putting summary key words in the margins.

2. They each tracked that they understood the content that had been presented.

3. They talked to friends who were in the same classes about lecture topics, which helped them to reinforce the ideas into long-term memory.

SUGGESTIONS FOR THE PROBLEM LECTURE

1. You are having difficulty understanding lecture material:
   - ☑ Complete the required reading before class.
   - ☑ Try to identify the headings and subheadings in your notes.
   - ☑ Ask for help after you have identified what is giving you difficulty.

2. You find you can't get everything down in your notes:
   - ☑ Check whether you really need to record every detail.
   - ☑ See if other students share your impression, and if so exchange notes to fill in gaps.
   - ☑ Be more strategic about using abbreviations in your notes.
   - ☑ Use pauses or repetition in the lecture to catch up with your note taking.

3. You seem to take down the "wrong" information:
   - ☑ Listen for headings to label the main themes.
   - ☑ Make sure that you are fully prepared for class and have done your readings.
   - ☑ Check any summary provided by the instructor (e.g., on the course website).
   - ☑ Tape a lecture (with permission) and listen to it again, so you can improve on your original notes with this review.

4. You find that you haven't reread your notes after several weeks in class:
   - ☑ Schedule some regular review time into your weekly study plan.
   - ☑ Check that your notes are attractive to go back to and, if not, work at producing a better set of notes in class.

5. After two or three weeks, you still can't follow the instructor:
   - ☑ Attend another lecture section **in addition to** the one to which you are assigned.
   - ☑ Discuss your problem with the instructor to see if he or she has any suggestions for you.
   - ☑ Ask another student in the course if you can see his or her notes from the last lecture.

THE PROS AND CONS OF TAPING LECTURES

One solution for dealing with problem lectures is to tape them and then listen to the tape again. If you are seriously considering this as an option, think about it carefully. Any time you are thinking of taping a class, you must first get permission from your instructor. Instructors vary in their attitude to having their lectures taped; some are very open to the idea while others will allow it only in special circumstances—for example, you have a documented disability that allows you the accommodation of taping classes, or you have a temporary problem like a broken arm.

The main advantage of taping a class is that you revisit that content while listening to the tape. If you use the tapes well, you can improve the notes you took in class, and this can be of great benefit especially if your difficulties are with the content or your instructor's pace of delivery. However, there are several reasons why taping a lecture should be the exception rather than the rule:

- It takes time to listen to the tape again—exactly the same amount of time as the original lecture. This will take away time from other crucial learning activities.
- You may be tempted to take notes that are too detailed—transcribing the tape rather than making summary notes of main ideas.
- Taping, especially in large classrooms, often produces a poor quality of sound and this can be frustrating to listen to.

If you do tape a class, aim to re-listen to the taped lecture as soon after class as possible, while it is still fresh in your mind. Also, make sure to take notes in the actual class, if at all possible, so that you modify existing notes as you listen to the tape. Try to limit your lecture taping to one course, and use this method only until you are feeling more confident about note taking in class.

WHAT ARE YOUR SUGGESTIONS FOR LECTURES?

If you were asked to help students with their note-taking issues, what strategies would you suggest? In this exercise on learning from lectures, suggested strategies for Fatima have been provided as a model. Complete the exercise by writing down three learning strategies for each of the problems that Bill, Brendan, and Winnie have presented to you.

In Fatima's astronomy course, she finds that the information in her text overlaps with her lectures. She would like to combine the two sources of material. What would be the best way of doing this?

1. _Fatima can read her text before class so that she is well prepared for class, but wait until after the lecture to make her summary notes from the text._

2. _After class and with her lecture notes open before her, she can make notes from the text that complement her lectures without too much overlap._

3. _She can use different colours of paper for her lecture and text notes and store them together in her binder, so that she can review them together for a test._

In Bill's business class at least half of each class is given over to discussion. He is not sure how to approach this type of class. Have you any suggestions on how he can improve his listening so that he can get the most benefit from these discussions?

1. _____

_____

2. _____

_____

3. _____

_____

Brendan is not happy with the notes he takes in his philosophy class. The professor speaks quickly and doesn't use a lot of visual aids. Brendan's notes have gaps in them, and he is never sure what the main ideas are. How can he improve on the notes he takes in class?

1. _____

_____

2. _____

_____

3. _____

_____

Winnie is a conscientious student who takes copious notes in all her lectures. After class she files them away until she reviews for exams. Suggest three review strategies that would lead to Winnie making better use of her notes.

1. _____

   _____

2. _____

   _____

3. _____

THE KEY ROLE OF LECTURE NOTES

This chapter emphasized the crucial role that you play in lectures, and how important it is for you to find the most efficient strategies for taking notes in class. Your notes should suit the course format, the structure of the content, and your own learning style. We recommend that you review your class notes within 24 hours of the lecture, periodically after that, and again just before a test. If you do have problems learning in class, first evaluate your own learning strategies to see if you can make changes to produce better results. Then, if you are still experiencing difficulty, talk to your instructor or to your learning skills counsellor.

Learning from lectures is closely linked to the topic of Chapter 5, "Learning from Textbooks," as both chapters focus on strategies for acquiring information. As you read about texts, think about the elements common to both learning from lectures and from texts.

WEB ALERT!

University of Guelph
Guelph, Ontario
www.learningcommons.uoguelph.ca
In the "QuickLinks" box (on the right of the screen), click on "Fastfacts Handouts" and then "Learning from Lectures," which is a review of key components including active listening, deciding what to write down, and note-taking mechanics. There is lots of good stuff in Guelph's Fastfacts!

C Consulting Limited

London, England

www.crazycolour.com/os

This is an interesting site, as it is geared for "Office Survival." In the list of handbooks (on the left side of the screen), scroll down to the "Working Efficiently Handbook." Then click on "Note Taking." From the options, make sure to check out both the "Cornell Note Taking System" and "Creating Your Own Abbreviations and Symbols."

Bucks County Community College

Newtown, Pennsylvania

www.bucks.edu/~specpop/visual-org.htm

The Basics of Effective Learning: Visual Organizers

CHAPTER ENDNOTES

1. Using a margin to add recall notes is based on the Cornell system of note taking. For more on this system, check the Web Alert! at the end of this chapter.
2. This paragraph is taken from *Psychology: The Adaptive Mind*, 2nd Cdn. ed. (p. 68), by J. S. Nairne, D. S. Lindsay, D. L. Paulus, & M. S. Smith, 2004, Scarborough, ON: Thomson Nelson.
3. Based on *Canadian Politics: Critical Approaches*, 4th ed., by R. Dyck, 2004, Scarborough, ON: Thomson Nelson.

Chapter 5

LEARNING FROM TEXTBOOKS

LEARNING OBJECTIVES

The purpose of this chapter is for you to:
- Assess your current reading strategies.
- Choose a reading approach appropriate for each course.
- Set realistic reading goals.
- Learn about an effective reading system—SQ4R.
- Improve your reading efficiency through building vocabulary and increasing reading speed.
- Learn how to skim and scan.

Text reading is one of the most important activities in any course. You will need to evaluate fairly quickly if your text covers the same information as the lectures, overlaps somewhat, or presents entirely complementary material. Will your instructor expect you to read the required pages before class and come to class knowing that background information? This is an important question to answer as you choose your approach to reading your text. This chapter suggests many reading strategies for you to think about and choose from as a Good Strategy User. As you read, think about each suggested strategy and decide if it will be part of your overall reading system. Choose to use only those strategies that are appropriate to your current reading task and that work well with your learning style. Begin with a self-assessment of your current approach to academic reading.

SELF-ASSESSMENT OF CURRENT APPROACH TO ACADEMIC READING

Read over the following statements, and think about your past reading assignments. How do these statements match your experience? Score each statement from 1 (this is not typical of me) up to 5 (this is very typical of me).

1. Each week I am clear about what I have to read.
2. I plan time each week to get my reading done.
3. I complete my readings within one week of their being assigned.
4. I always have definite goals in mind when I sit down to read.
5. I look over each chapter before beginning to read.
6. I pay a lot of attention to headings and highlighted text.
7. I always read the captions for illustrations and any marginal notes.
8. I read in a place where I can give my full attention to the task.
9. I take a short break when I begin to get tired and soon go back to the task with increased attention.
10. I think about how the text and lecture complement each other.
11. I make a record of the key points, either by highlighting the text or by making summary notes.
12. If I don't understand what I am reading, I get help from another student or my instructor.

_____   13. To structure my summary notes, I include in them all of the headings and subheadings from the chapter.

_____   14. I periodically review my highlighting or summary notes for each chapter so that I limit forgetting.

_____   15. I try to predict from my readings what might be on the next test.

My Total Score _____

EVALUATING YOUR RESPONSES

Each of the above statements is a sound strategy that can help you learn effectively from texts. As there are 15 statements in this list, each ranked from 1–5, your total score can range anywhere from a low of 15 to a high of 75. If you score at the low end of this range—say, below 30—then you need to work on your strategies for learning from texts. If you score at the high end—say, above 60—then you have already established a sound approach to text reading.

THE ROLE OF THE TEXT IN THE COURSE

> Nick failed his first psychology test. He was very upset and angry, and he threw a thick wad of notes taken from the text onto his desk. "I really studied for that test," he said. "I put in hours of work, made all these notes, and my mark was 40 percent—a failing grade and well below the class average."

As the above scenario illustrates, Nick has a real dilemma: he worked hard for his psychology test, putting in many hours reading and recording from his text, but he still failed the test. However, the other side of Nick's story is that he did not like 8:30 a.m. classes and so had not attended many of his psychology lectures. The text in that course covered only a small part of the lecture content—something that Nick did not realize—and so despite spending hours reading his text Nick was poorly prepared for the test.

AVOIDING READING DILEMMAS

By carefully considering the role of the text in each course you take, you can avoid making the same mistake as Nick. Think about the role of the text in one of your courses and answer the following questions.

Name of course: _____

1. How much reading is assigned each week in this course, and how long do I estimate it will take me to complete it?

   Approximate number of pages: _____

   Amount of time I need: _____

2. How much overlap is there in the content of lectures and text; that is, how similar or dissimilar is the content from both sources?

   _____

   _____

   _____

3. What will I need to know after reading my text—all main ideas and supporting details for multiple-choice tests or major themes with some key examples for essay questions?

   _____

   _____

   _____

GETTING TO KNOW YOUR TEXT

When you begin a new course and before your first reading assignment, browse through the text. Find out about your text's background, and evaluate the content and organization of the book. Texts often reflect the time and place in which they were written as well as any personal biases or perspectives of the authors. Be aware of this background with any texts you read, and you will be well prepared to evaluate the content. Use Box 5.1, "Text Overview," as a guide as you get to know one of your own texts.

SET YOUR READING GOALS

As you begin a text assignment, you need to set goals for the task. Remember that Chapter 2, "Resources for Strategic Learners," discussed setting content-oriented and strategy-oriented goals as well as time-management goals. Ask yourself, *"What do I have to read, and how will I approach it?"* and *"How much time will I give to this task?"*

BOX 5.1   Text Overview

The Preface

☑ Who wrote the book?

☑ How recently was it published?

☑ Where was it written?

☑ What is the perspective/bias of the author(s)?

Table of Contents

☑ What topics are covered and in what order?

☑ What is the logic behind that particular order of topics?

☑ How do the chapter topics match the lectures?

☑ Is the book subdivided into major sections or parts—if so, what are their titles?

☑ What information is included at the front and back of the text: preface, glossary, appendix, and index?

Content and Organization of Each Chapter

☑ Are the chapters divided into sections with subheadings, and, if so, can the sections be easily identified?

☑ What illustrative materials are used: pictures, case studies, figures, tables?

☑ How are key ideas and definitions highlighted: **bold text** or *italics*?

☑ Is there a glossary of key words?

☑ Are questions posed to get the reader thinking?

☑ Is there important information in the margins?

The time-management goal is crucial to reading texts. If you give yourself an open-ended amount of time to complete the task, you will find that there is no urgency to get finished and you may spend much longer than necessary. Initially set yourself a goal, such as 10 pages of text in one hour. Watch the clock and push ahead to get finished in the planned time. If it is an impossible task, then you will need to reconsider and set a different time goal next time. You can train yourself to be a faster and more efficient reader if you are a goal setter. Practise goal setting for reading by setting some goals now for completing this current chapter, "Learning from Textbooks."

My Short-Term Reading Goals:

The reading task I have to get done is:

<u>I have to finish this chapter, "Learning from Textbooks"</u>

This is how I intend to proceed:

_____

_____

_____

I plan to spend this amount of time to complete this task:

_____

SQ4R: A SYSTEM FOR READING TEXTS[1]

SQ4R is an acronym for the five steps in an effective reading system. It stands for:

- Survey
- Question
- Read and Reflect
- Record
- Review

SURVEY

You should spend only a few minutes surveying a chapter before beginning to read. You will activate your background knowledge, ask important questions, and make an outline of the headings of the chapter into a useful review tool.

Activate Your Background Knowledge

Look at the chapter title, think about its theme, and ask yourself, *"What do I already know about this topic?"* If your instructor has presented information in class that is relevant to the chapter, reread your lecture notes.

Ask Important Questions

- Chapter title *(What is this whole chapter about?)*
- Headings and subheadings *(What are the main topics, and how are they organized?)*

- Introduction and summary *(What do they emphasize?)*
- Captions *(What is illustrated in the pictures, figures, and tables?)*
- Bibliography *(What are the additional materials on this topic?)*

Make an Outline of the Headings of the Chapter

Some texts provide an outline or overview of the main headings for each chapter. Paying close attention to this outline helps you to set up a structure for the chapter in your long-term memory. As you look over the main headings, ask yourself, *"What is this chapter about?"* If your text doesn't include chapter outlines, make one for yourself as you read each chapter.

Look at the example in Box 5.2,[2] and you will see that the outline emphasizes the relationship between the main headings and the subheadings. As you look over the topics in this example, notice how the first section defines the topic of "Deviance," the next five sections cover different theoretical perspectives on "Crime and Deviance," while the last three sections look at general aspects of the topic. You might expect some compare/contrast questions on a test based on this chapter.

If your text provides outlines for each chapter, you can photocopy them and staple them together. This makes a useful learning tool, because you can review the outlines periodically to recite and recall key points from memory.

BOX 5.2   Chapter Outline Sheet

Chapter 7—Crime and Deviance

1. What Is Deviance?

2. Functionalist Perspectives on Crime and Deviance
   - Strain Theory: Goals and the means to achieve them
   - Opportunity Theory: Access to legitimate opportunities
   - Control Theory: Social bonding

3. Symbolic Interactionist Perspectives on Crime & Deviance
   - Differential association theory
   - Labelling theory

4. Critical Perspectives on Crime and Deviance
   - The conflict approach

5. Feminist Perspectives on Crime and Deviance

6. Postmodern Perspectives on Crime and Deviance

7. Crime Classification
   - How the law classifies crime
   - How sociologists classify crime
   - Crime statistics
   - Street crimes and criminals

8. The Criminal Justice System
   - The police
   - The courts
   - Punishment
   - Restorative justice
   - Community corrections

9. Deviance & Crime in the Future

QUESTION

In the previous paragraphs you were directed to ask questions as you survey your texts. Questions play a key role in an effective reading system, and each of the six steps in this reading system includes questions. Asking questions is one reading strategy that is applicable to all reading assignments.

READ AND REFLECT

When you read a text, your goals are much broader than simply to understand what you are reading at that moment in time; you also want to *remember* what you are reading and apply the ideas to future tests and assignments. Effective reading is a complex learning process, and so you will need to use a variety of strategies to attain your goals: strategies to construct meaning out of the words and visual images on the page; strategies for connecting new concepts together and to your existing knowledge base; strategies for monitoring that you understand what you are reading. Strategies for reading and reflecting operate together to help you achieve your reading goals.

Read the Subheadings

As you begin to read each subsection of the chapter, pay particular attention to its heading, and ask yourself, *"What is this section about?"* As you read, check to see if your prediction was correct. You will find that some headings are very descriptive, making it easy to predict the content; others are not so transparent and you will have to read on to get the gist of the material.

Pick Up Clues from the Text Layout

Text layout provides many clues to key ideas, and can answer the question, *"What hints is the text giving to me?"* **Bold** or *italics* in text are there for emphasis. Illustrative material, organized in charts, graphs, figures, boxes, and tables, is likely to be key information. Also, marginal notes are there for a purpose, so read them carefully.

Seek Out Main Ideas

Although reading to identify main ideas is not an easy task, it is very important that you develop this skill of discriminating between the most important key ideas and the supporting details. One way to do this is to read one paragraph or a few paragraphs (no highlighting and no taking notes at this point!), and then ask yourself, *"What was most important here?"* If this is how you habitually approach reading from text, you will become skilful at identifying main ideas, which is so critical to academic success.

Rephrase What You Read Using Your Own Words

When you have finished reading a paragraph or set of paragraphs, ask yourself *"What did this say?"* If you can paraphrase and summarize the text into your own words, you will be achieving two important reading goals: understanding the information and putting that information into long-term memory.

Build the Big Picture

Reflect on how all of the individual ideas fit together to form a big picture. Ask yourself, *"How does this new text information fit with what I am hearing in lectures and with my broader understanding of this topic?"* The more connections you make, the better you will understand and remember the information.

Form Visual Images

Many topics bring visual images to mind. For example, in the outline of the sociology chapter (Box 5.2), the term "crime statistics" can trigger thoughts and images about news stories you have read about in a newspaper or seen on television. Visual images are much easier to remember than abstract ideas, and so as you read, ask yourself, *"Can I see my own examples to illustrate these concepts?"*

Monitor Your Comprehension

Periodically, as you read, ask yourself, *"Is this making sense to me?"* As academic work is intended to challenge learners so they can reach higher levels of understanding, you may find that some sections of your text take more effort. It may take time before everything falls into place, and you may need to read over difficult sections several times or wait until the lecture to clarify some of the ideas. If you do have continuing difficulty, seek out help from friends, from your instructor, or from student support personnel such as your learning skills counsellor.

Monitor Your Emotional Response to the Text

Maintain a positive attitude toward the text as you ask, *"Am I enjoying reading this text?"* Attitude is an important part of being a Good Strategy User and can strongly influence your ability to understand and remember key information.

RECORD

Making a record of the most important points from your readings is important both for your memory of the information and for reviewing for tests. A well-taken set of summary notes is an invaluable review aid. Summary notes take less time to review, as they highlight the most important ideas. Consider the following text-recording strategies, but note that you need not use them all! You need to select recording strategies that will be effective for you and aid your comprehension and retention of the information:

Underline or Highlight to Facilitate Later Review

If you choose to highlight or underline main ideas in your text, there is only one way to do it well. Read to understand first—at least a few paragraphs—before stopping, thinking, and then selecting ideas to highlight or underline. In addition to plain highlighting or underlining, you can use a variety of symbols to highlight key information—brackets, boxes, asterisks, circles, and so on. If a sequence of ideas is presented, you can add numbers onto the text itself (see Figure 5.1).[3] Note that if you over-highlight, then nothing stands out. So, *get in the habit of highlighting quite sparingly.*

It is usually quite difficult to study from highlighting by itself. It needs to be used in conjunction with either of the next two recording methods: marginal notes or summary notes.

Add Key Words/Brief Notes to the Margin of the Text

Some modern texts have very wide margins that provide plenty of space in which to add some of your own notes. Adding notes to the margin can be an effective system, especially for very detailed texts such as some psychology or biology texts. When reviewing for tests using your text, the notes you wrote in the margins may trigger instant recall, or you can reread that section by the note.

Make a Separate Set of Summary Notes

- If you choose to make summary notes from your text, you can either write them by hand or use your computer.
- Don't copy exactly from the text; paraphrase the summary points into your own words. This forces you to take an active role in checking your comprehension as you read.
- Organize your summary notes under the same set of subheadings as in the text.
- Structure your notes with indents, bulleted or numbered lists, and underlining to emphasize structure. Note that Figure 5.2, which summarizes the text in Figure 5.1, incorporates all of the above suggestions.
- Avoid the common mistake of taking too many notes. Also, think hard about how you will remember what you record. Many students end up with a great set of notes on paper but can't remember anything they read. If the strategy of taking summary notes is to work, you have to put in the time to learn what is in your notes.

Other Methods

- Create graphic organizers to display relationships among main ideas.
- Make up test questions.
- Make your own glossary list of key concepts with definitions.

REVIEW

As there is usually a lot of time between learning and testing, forgetting can be a very real problem. Therefore, review is a necessary step in effective reading. The following review strategies cover time management as well as recitation and self-testing:

- ☑ Review immediately following your first reading; this should not take long because the information is still fresh in your memory.
- ☑ Plan time every two weeks or so to engage in a quick review of the chapters. This will keep previously learned information fresh in your memory as the amount increases.
- ☑ Before a test, set aside a specific amount of time to spend in careful, thorough review.
- ☑ Cover the page. Recite silently or aloud the important points that you need to remember. If you cannot remember, recheck the page and try again.

FIGURE 5.1   An Example of Highlighted Text with Marginal Notes

How Sociologists Classify Crime

Sociologists categorize crimes based on (how) they are committed and (how) society views the offences. We will examine |four| types: (1) street crime; (2) occupational, or white-collar, and corporate crime; (3) organized crime; and (4) political crime. As you read about these types of crime, ask yourself how you feel about them. Should each be a crime? How severe should the sanctions be against each type?

3 TYPES

1. **STREET CRIME** When people think of crime, the images that most commonly come to mind are of *street crime,* which includes all (violent) crime, certain (property) crimes, and certain (morals) crimes. Examples are robbery, assault, and break and enter. These are the crimes that occupy most of the time and attention of the criminal justice system. Obviously, all street crime does not occur on the street; it frequently occurs in the home, workplace, and other locations.

a) (Violent crime) consists of actions involving force or the threat of force against others, including murder, sexual assault, robbery, and aggravated

egs assault. Violent crimes are probably the most anxiety-provoking of all criminal behaviour. Victims often are physically injured or even lose their lives; the psychological trauma may last for years after the event (Parker, 1995). Violent crime receives the most sustained attention from law enforcement officials and the media (see Warr, 1995). And, while much attention may be given to the violent stranger, the vast majority of violent crime victims actually are injured by someone

* whom they know: family members, friends, neighbours, or co-workers (Silverman and Kennedy, 1993).

b) (Property crimes) include break and enter, theft,

egs motor vehicle theft, and arson. While violent crime receives the most publicity, property crime is much more common. In most property crimes, the

* primary motive is to obtain money or some other desired valuable.

c) (Morals crimes) involve an illegal action voluntarily engaged in by the participants, such as prostitution, illegal gambling, the private use of

egs. illegal drugs, and illegal pornography. Many people assert that such conduct should not be labelled as a crime; these offences often are referred to as "victimless crimes" because they involve exchanges of

* illegal goods or services among willing adults (Schur, 1965).

However, morals crimes can include children ***** and adolescents as well as adults. Young children and adolescents may unwillingly become child pornography "stars" or prostitutes. Members of juvenile gangs often find selling drugs to be a lucrative business in which getting addicted and/or arrested is merely an occupational hazard.

2. **OCCUPATIONAL AND CORPORATE CRIME** Although Edwin Sutherland (1949) developed the concept of white-collar crime over fifty years ago, it was not until the 1980s that the public really became aware of its nature. **(Occupational or white-collar) a)** **crime consists of illegal activities committed by people in the course of their employment or in dealing with their financial affairs.**

At the heart of much white-collar crime is a violation of positions of trust in business or government (Shapiro, 1990). These activities include pilfering (employee theft of company property or profits), soliciting bribes or kickbacks, and embez- **egs** zling. In the past decade, computers have created even greater access to such illegal practices. Some white-collar criminals set up businesses for the sole purpose of victimizing the general public, engaging in activities such as land swindles, securities thefts, and consumer fraud.

In addition to acting for their own financial benefit, some white-collar offenders become involved in criminal conspiracies designed to improve the market share or profitability of their companies. This is known as (corporate crime— **b)** **illegal acts committed by corporate employees on behalf of the corporation and with its support.** Examples include antitrust violations; false advertising; infringements on patents, copyrights, and **egs.** trademarks; price-fixing; and financial fraud. These crimes are a result of deliberate decisions made by corporate personnel to enhance resources or profits at the expense of competitors, consumers, and the general public.

The cost of white-collar and corporate crimes ******* far exceeds that of street crime. Gabor (1994) reports that tax evasion costs Canadians about $30 billion a year. In one of the world's biggest white-collar crimes, investors in Calgary's Bre-X gold-mining company lost around $5 billion when it was learned that geologist Michael de Guzman had salted core samples with gold to make a worthless mining property look like the world's biggest gold find. At the individual level, while few bank robbers get away with more than a few thousand dollars, Julius Melnitzer (a London, Ontario,

FIGURE 5.2   An Example of Summary Notes

HOW SOCIOLOGISTS CLASSIFY CRIME

1. Street Crime

   a) Violent Crime e.g., murder, assault
   - creates much anxiety
   - much police attention
   - most victims know attacker
   b) Property Crime e.g., break & enter, arson, car theft
   - much more common than violent crime
   c) Morals Crimes e.g., prostitution, drugs, pornography
   - illegal actions engaged in by willing participants
   - can hurt others e.g., children in pornography

2. Occupational & Corporate Crime

   a) Occupational – on job activities e.g., theft, bribes, kickbacks, embezzlement
   - violation of trust
   - for personal gain
   b) Corporate Crime e.g., antitrust violations, false advertising, patent infringement, price fixing etc.
   - deliberate actions to enhance resources or profits at expense of others.

N.B. Cost of occup/corp crimes much higher than cost of street crimes. egs in Canada are Bre-X, Calgary & Julius Melnitzer – London, ON

☑ When you have some spare time (at the bus stop or while changing classes), recall the organization of a chapter by reciting the subheadings. You do not need to have the text or your summary notes at hand when you practise recalling key information.

☑ Think about the glossary or key word list that you prepared. How many of those words can you recall? Can you define them and give examples?

☑ Use scrap paper or your computer to practise writing down critical information from memory.

☑ Make up your own test questions, and use them to test yourself at a later date.

☑ If your text has questions, make sure that you can answer them from memory.

☑ Recheck any concepts highlighted in the text in bold or italics, and make sure that you can define the terms and explain how they fit into the big picture.

☑ If old exams are available, rehearse by simulating the real test. Give yourself a time limit and answer the questions as though you were writing a real test.

☑ Organize or join a study group with a few classmates, and find ways to test each other.

☑ If your text has a study guide, answer the questions in it.

IMPROVE YOUR READING EFFICIENCY

Two of the most important components of improving your efficiency as a reader are building your vocabulary and increasing your reading speed.

STRATEGIES FOR BUILDING VOCABULARY

- If you come across a new word, first think about it in context. What do you suppose it might mean?
- Have a good dictionary at hand, and look up any word that is new to you.
- Keep a running list of new words, and look over them periodically. It is useful to have a small and easily transportable notebook for this.
- Use newly learned words by including them in both your written and spoken language.
- When you are in a lecture, listen for words that are new to you and write them down in your notes. Many instructors have an expanded vocabulary and are a great resource for your own vocabulary improvement.
- Read, read, read. As you read newspapers, magazines, books, and information on the Internet, watch out for new vocabulary. The more you read and see new words, the more you will be able to recognize and use them yourself.

- Expand your vocabulary every day from people around you—family and friends, as well as the television, Internet, and movies.
- Identify the roots in new words, and these will give you some of the basic meaning. Many words in the English language have their roots in Latin (L) or Greek (G). For each of the following word roots, think of one or more words that might be used in your courses and that incorporate(s) the meaning of the root:

arbor (L) tree	blast (G) bud	cand (L) brilliant
dorm (L) sleep	endo (G) inner	frat (L) brother
geo (G) earth	hyra (G) water	infuse (L) pour in
ject (L) throw	kilo (G) thousand	lamin (L) layer
mes (G) middle	neo (G) new	omni (L) all
ped (L) foot	ped (G) child	quasi (L) almost
recit (L) read out	saga (L) shrewd	tach (G) quickly
ubiqu (L) everywhere	vis (L) see	viv (L) living
xer (G) dry	yper (G) over	zyl (G) wood

STRATEGIES FOR INCREASING READING SPEED

- Read in a good location where you can concentrate on the task.
- Be physically comfortable—but not too comfortable—while you are reading.
- Plan to read when you will not be too tired.
- Set some time limits for the task at hand. Work toward these limits that you have set for yourself.
- Survey your reading assignment before reading in depth. The headings and other highlights in the text will set up expectations and boost your reading speed.
- Consciously think about how your eyes skim over the words from left to right and try to maintain that sweep across the lines.
- Guide your eye movements with a finger or a pencil held at the side of the page. Gradually move it down the page as you read. It will give you a marker to aim toward and will help to direct your eyes in an efficient path across the text.
- As your eyes move across a line, focus more on the key words such as nouns and verbs. You do not always have to read every word to get a good sense of the material. However, more difficult material will require that you slow down and process more completely.
- Monitor how much you subvocalize as you read. Subvocalization occurs when you say the words to yourself. One way to limit this is to place something—a pen, maybe—between your teeth as you read.

LEARN TO SKIM AND SCAN

For most of your text reading, you will have to read thoroughly and methodically so that you have a good grasp of very specific details that may show up on tests. However, you will have other reading assignments that can benefit from a more expansive approach. For example, you may have to read a variety of materials for a tutorial or case study discussion; you may be checking out possible sources for a seminar presentation or an essay or research paper. For this type of task, skimming and scanning for relevant information are appropriate and sophisticated techniques, and ones you will find very useful in the years long after being a student.

SKIMMING

You skim a text to find specific information without having to read every word. There is no one method for skimming, as the structure of the material itself may dictate how best you do it. If you can develop confidence in the technique, you will be amazed at how successful it can be. In as short a time as 20 minutes, you can skim at least 50 pages and have a reasonable and useable sense of the subject matter.

- Start by looking at the title and any subtitles to get an overview of the topic.
- Read the introduction and conclusion to see if the writer has summarized key points.
- Skim for anything that is highlighted in a different font or displayed in pictures or diagrams.
- If available, check the glossary of key terms for the major concepts in the chapter.
- Read the first sentences of each paragraph, or randomly choose paragraphs to read.

SCANNING

Scanning is the method to use when you have something specific in mind that you want to find out about and that you are scanning for. The best way to scan is to think of relevant key words and phrases before you begin. Because you keep these words and phrases in mind, they pop out of the text and you locate them quickly. You can then make a judgment on whether the text is worth reading later in greater depth. Tables of contents of books and abstracts of journal articles lend themselves particularly well to scanning.

For example, you might be in the early stages of researching a paper on John G. Diefenbaker as Prime Minister of Canada from 1957–63. You have taken a dozen books off the library shelf and are trying to decide which four you will check out and take home with you. In addition to scanning for the name Diefenbaker, you might scan for key words and phrases associated with some of his accomplishments: Ellen Fairclough (first Canadian woman federal cabinet minister), Canadian Bill of Rights, native peoples get the vote, old-age pensions expanded, simultaneous translation in the House of Commons.

WHAT ARE YOUR SUGGESTIONS FOR TEXT READING?

If you were asked to help students with their text-reading issues, what strategies would you suggest? In this exercise, suggested strategies for Mike have been provided as a model. Complete the exercise by writing down three learning strategies for each of the problems that Natasha, Meghan, and Ellis have presented to you.

Mike is taking his first psychology class and is finding that the weekly assigned readings are taking far too long to complete. He always takes notes from his readings to aid his memory. He would like some suggestions on how he can get through his reading assignments more efficiently. Where can he start?

1. Mike can first check with some of his classmates to see if he is in fact taking longer than the average for this task.

2. He can check on the role of the text in the course. If there is a lot of overlap with the lecture material, he may be able to take fewer notes from the text.

3. Mike can try reading several pages without taking notes and then stopping to summarize those pages. This may be faster than taking notes as he reads.

Natasha is a really serious student who aims to get the best results out of her text reading. She wants to find a sound approach that will optimize her comprehension of the material. What strategies can you suggest that can lead to excellent comprehension for Natasha?

1. _____

_____

2. _____

_____

3. _____

_____

Meghan has a lot of course reading in her program. She makes herself sit down to read at least three hours each evening, one evening per course. She wants to find an effective and efficient way to record information as she reads. Can you suggest some effective strategies for recording main ideas from text?

1. _____

_____

2. _____

_____

3. _____

_____

Ellis does not like reading, as he finds that forgetting is a real problem for him. What are some ways that Ellis can reinforce his learning from text?

1. _____

_____

2. _____

_____

3. _____

_____

A PERSONALIZED APPROACH TO READING

The knowledge you acquire from texts plays a vital role in your academic success. It is, therefore, essential that you find a way to read texts that is both manageable and effective for *each* of your courses. One of the mistakes that many students make is to read every text in exactly the same way. Your reading assignments can vary greatly in the amount of time required and in the amount of detail you expect to retain after reading, and as a Good Strategy User you will tailor the way you read a text to match its specific demands. For any reading assignment, it is useful to consider planning your reading strategies around a reading system for comprehending and recording main ideas from your texts. In this chapter you were introduced to such a system: SQ4R.

With some key strategies in place for identifying and using resources, managing your time, and learning from lectures and texts, you are off to a smart start in your academic experience. The next part of this book goes beyond the basics to explore other academic areas of importance to many students. It begins by looking at a topic of universal interest: effective memory.

WEB ALERT!

University of New Brunswick
Fredericton, New Brunswick
http://extend.unb.ca/wss/actitext.htm
Active Reading Strategies

Douglas College
New Westminster, British Columbia
www.douglas.bc.ca/learning/selfhelp.html
Follow the links in "Self-Help Materials" to "Spelling and Vocabulary," then to "Remembering New Words: Improving Your Vocabulary."

Dartmouth College
Hanover, New Hampshire
www.dartmouth.edu/~acskills/success/reading.html
Reading Your Textbooks Effectively and Efficiently. This covers SQ3R.

CHAPTER ENDNOTES

1. Based on SQ3R—first suggested by Dr. Frances P. Robinson. See *Effective Reading*, by F. P. Robinson, 1962, New York: Harper and Brothers.
2. The example is based on Chapter 7, "Crime and Deviance," in the introductory text *Sociology in Our Times,* 3rd Cdn. ed., by D. Kendall, J. Lothian Murray, & R. Linden, 2004, Scarborough, ON: Thomson Nelson.
3. A sample page from Chapter 7, "Crime and Deviance," in the introductory text *Sociology in Our Times,* 3rd Cdn. ed., by D. Kendall, J. Lothian Murray, & R. Linden, 2004, Scarborough, ON: Thomson Nelson.

Part 3

GOING BEYOND THE BASICS

Chapter 6

EFFECTIVE MEMORY

LEARNING OBJECTIVES

The purpose of this chapter is for you to:

- Learn about three memory systems and their relevance to you as a learner.
- Explore the concept of memory structures through an exercise.
- Apply the ideas of structuring information to your own studies.
- Learn how to improve your memory storage.

Students commonly report problems with memory. Many describe how they can understand new ideas, but later the information just doesn't stick. They also commonly report that their friends can remember everything without any effort at all, and often get higher grades than they do without, seemingly, having studied much at all. While there are undoubtedly differences among students in the ease with which information is retained, there are strategies that you can apply to improve your retention over the long term. To be able to apply effective memory strategies, you need first to understand some current theory about memory that can help to explain memory problems.

This chapter begins by examining how three types of memory are thought to operate together and what this implies for you as a learner. It then goes on to explore ways in which memory is stored to improve retrieval. The main purpose of this chapter is to have you relate the theory about memory systems to your own learning experience. As you read, ask yourself the following questions: *"How does this theory reflect my own way of studying? In light of these theories, what changes do I need to make to the way in which I study? What do I need to do to build these ideas into my own learning strategies?"*

MEMORY SYSTEMS

Educators distinguish three memory systems operating together, each with distinct characteristics and functions (see Figure 6.1).[1] They are described very briefly here, focusing on the major implications for your personal control over your own learning processes.

- Sensory Memory
- Short-Term Memory
- Long-Term Memory

SENSORY MEMORY

Your senses—sight, hearing, touch, taste, smell, and sense of position—register information from the environment, but only for an instant. It is then either forgotten or is passed to your short-term memory as a conscious thought. How is this significant to you as a learner? Well, you might view sensory memory as a critical gateway through which information must pass in order to be available to your short-term memory. For information to register in short-term memory, you must attend to and concentrate on it.

In everyday life, if you could register all of the stimuli available to your sensory-memory system, your senses would become overloaded. When you sit at a desk processing some lecture notes, for example, you do not usually notice the pressure of your feet on the floor or hear background noises around you, such as a fan or traffic outside.

FIGURE 6.1   A Theoretical View of Memory

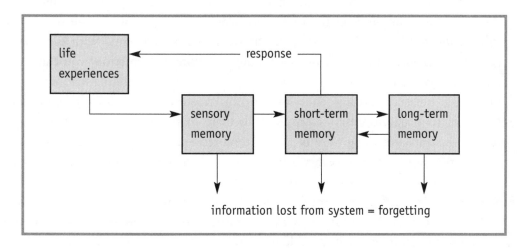

To be a Good Strategy User, you need to develop the ability to limit your attention to critical and relevant stimuli. Much of what your sensory memory does register is related to goals you set. In other words, your short-term goals have a profound effect on the information that passes from your sensory to your short-term memory.

SHORT-TERM MEMORY

Short-term memory is sometimes referred to as working memory, because it is here that you actively work to make sense of and respond to stimuli entering from the sensory memory environment or from knowledge you retrieve from long-term storage. Two limitations of short-term memory are critical to you as a learner: The first is that short-term memory has a very small capacity—only about five to seven items of information can be held at any one time. This means that when new information enters short-term memory, it often displaces what is already there. For example, switching between the simultaneous activities of listening and taking notes in a lecture can be very difficult if the lecture is fast paced. Unless you maintain some internal dialogue involving repetition of a critical phrase you wish to record, it is displaced by new information, and you quickly forget the earlier information. The second limitation of short-term memory is that you lose information very quickly by forgetting, unless you process the information further in some way (e.g., by reciting a telephone number over and over again in your head if something stops you from dialling the number immediately). If you are to minimize forgetting from short-term memory as you learn, you need to use strategies that help you overcome these limitations. Here are two general strategies that can help:

1. **Limit the amount of information you process at one time:** Try to work with about five important pieces of information for a few minutes at a time. In reading a textbook, for example, read the five or so paragraphs that typically fall under one subheading then stop and summarize the main points associated with each paragraph; in preparing for an exam that requires recalling information, you can work on reciting the five or so main points that fall under one subheading before moving on to the next subheading; in essay writing, create an outline with about four subtopics then develop each subtopic with three to five main points. The key to using this strategy is to be wary of that natural tendency to try to handle too much information at one time, whether it be reading or reviewing a whole chapter in "one go" or trying to write an essay from start to finish.

2. **Summarize important information quickly:** As you process information, you typically need to make some kind of written summary of the important points. If you can do this quickly, you will be able to handle courses that cover large amounts of information. Therefore, it is very useful to develop quick ways to summarize important points in writing when you are taking notes in a lecture, making a summary of a text chapter, or recording some research. You can do this by learning to use abbreviations (as presented in Chapter 4, "Learning from Lectures"), and, when appropriate, by using graphic organizers such as diagrams or tables.

LONG-TERM MEMORY

This is the component of memory that stores all of the information you have learned. Much like a very large library or computer, it has an immense storage capacity. However, it also resembles a library or computer in the sense that very careful storage and retrieval procedures are needed so that information is not lost inside the system. Unfortunately, many students do not have conscious and reliable procedures for information storage and retrieval and so forget a lot of information. The remainder of this chapter deals with strategies to help you move information from short-term memory to long-term memory in a way that allows for efficient information storage and retrieval.

STRUCTURING INFORMATION TO ENHANCE STORAGE

The way in which you critically select and structure new information to store in long-term memory is probably the most important contributing factor to your success as a student. If you are enjoying academic success, there are likely two important aspects to the way in which you have stored information in your long-term memory:

1. **Your storage of information is likely to be hierarchical.** This means that you place a small amount of crucial information at the highest level (such as a main heading or key idea), and then you place a larger number of supporting details at successively lower levels. Researchers have aptly described this storage pattern as a *pyramid of information.*[2]

2. **You make connections among these items of stored information.** You evaluate the connections from one level of the pyramid to another level, and you also make connections among items of information that are all on the same level.

To illustrate these two points, you could structure a hierarchical summary of the previous section of this chapter by placing "Memory Systems" at the top level of the pyramid, then placing the three different types of memory at the next lower level, and finally placing important details for each type at the lowest level. You could then make connections among all of the items of information by thinking about how the three memory systems work together. A structured memory, such as this one, would facilitate your efficient retrieval of the information at a later time.

If you are having difficulty remembering information in a particular course, it may well be that your storage of that information in long-term memory shows little structure. Instead, you are probably trying to memorize many isolated pieces of information. This lack of structure makes your efficient retrieval of information very difficult.

To get a sense of the power of structured memories, try the following exercise. Read the passage below as though you were going to have to remember it for a test.

> The procedure is actually quite simple. First you arrange things into different groups. Of course, one pile may be sufficient depending on how much there is to do. If you have to go somewhere else due to lack of facilities, that is the next step, otherwise you are pretty well set. It is important not to overdo things. That is, it is better to do too few things at once than too many. In the short run this may not seem important but complications can arise. A mistake can be expensive as well. At first the whole procedure will seem complicated. Soon, however, it will become just another fact of life. It is difficult to foresee any end to the necessity for this task in the immediate future, but one never can tell. After the procedure is completed one arranges the materials into different groups again. Then they can be put into their appropriate places. Eventually they will be used once more and the whole cycle will then have to be repeated. However, that is part of life.[3]

You may have found on first reading that this passage did not seem to make much sense and read as a string of unrelated facts. If so, you would have found it difficult to memorize the information that it contains. But wait! Give this passage a title—"Doing the Laundry"—and note what happens. The title helps you to structure the information, and the passage now makes sense. The title of "Doing the Laundry" has retrieved from your long-term memory a relevant **memory structure** connected to this particular activity.

Your retrieved memory structure organizes information on three levels: 1. It gives you a TITLE; that is, "Doing the Laundry." 2. It activates GENERAL CATEGORIES of information appropriate to the activity of doing the laundry, including a *purpose* for the activity, *component parts,* a logical *sequence of events,* and a *conclusion.* 3. You can then use each of these general categories to guide your recall of SPECIFIC DETAILS; for example, the specific details for *component parts* in doing the laundry are 1. dirty clothes, 2. detergent, and 3. a washing machine.

On rereading the passage with its title of "Doing the Laundry," you are now able to organize the information in this passage very quickly. Your short-term memory compares the information from this passage with an established memory structure that you retrieved from long-term memory. The information in the passage matches clearly with your existing memory structure for "Doing the Laundry" and, therefore, it becomes very easy to remember.

CREATING MEMORY STRUCTURES

Organizing academic information into memory structures is crucial to effective learning. Without these structures your memory is soon overwhelmed by details. Some of the course material you learn matches quickly with your existing memory structures, just as this laundry example did. Most information, however, will be quite new to you, and so you will need to organize it into new memory structures. This is not actually so difficult. As explained earlier, memory structures can be viewed as having three levels of information, and so to create useful memory structures you need to pay attention to each level in turn:

- The Title
- General Categories of Information
- Specific Details That Fit under Each of the General Categories

THE TITLE

It is very important that you attach a title to each memory structure you build, for without a title the entire memory structure can be very easily forgotten. Titles for memory structures are typically the headings or subheadings from your lecture or textbook.

General Categories of Information

This is the most crucial—and often most overlooked—level in any memory structure. For each topic you encounter in a course, you will want to summarize and organize the important details using general categories of information appropriate to that kind of course material. If you are like many students, you may already watch out for definitions—which represent just one category of information—but not track consciously for any other categories. This means that you just guess at what other details are important. Sometimes this unconscious selection and organization of details can work because you have an intuitive "feel" for the material. However, intuitive feel can let you down and, as a Good Strategy User, you will want to use a strategy that is much more systematic and reliable.

The general categories of information in a memory structure are similar to categories of information you maintain for friends. For example, for each friend you would want to record details under such categories as 1. telephone number, 2. mailing address, 3. e-mail address, 4. birthday, and so on. So it is with each topic you encounter in a course; you will want to summarize and organize the important details you have to learn into the general categories of information appropriate to that kind of course material.

Listed in Table 6.1 are some suggested general categories of information you can use with different types of courses. Note that these are suggested categories only, and you may wish to add to or subtract from these lists. You might make a list, on a sheet of paper or flashcard, of the likely appropriate general categories of information for each course you are taking. Then you will be ready to use these categories of information to guide your selection of specific details in those courses.

Specific Details That Fit under Each of the General Categories

Review your list of appropriate general categories of information before you attend a lecture or read a textbook. Then try to listen or read for specific details to match your chosen category of information. For example, you may notice that your sociology textbook explains a particular theory by defining some new terms, then gives you the essentials of the theory followed by some evidence to back up the theory. Summarizing this passage is then much easier, because you have only to extract the few phrases that contain the key specific details for each general category.

An Example of How to Create a Memory Structure

Many students find biology courses quite challenging because each topic typically covers a lot of complex material that requires considerable memorization. Here is an example of how you can use the strategy of creating a memory structure to make the learning of a topic in biology much easier.

TABLE 6.1   Suggested General Categories

TYPE OF COURSE	SUGGESTED GENERAL CATEGORIES OF INFORMATION
Concepts or theories in the social sciences and humanities, business, science, etc.	1. Essence of the concept or theory 2. Definitions of any new terms 3. Evidence and examples in support of the concept 4. Conclusions 5. Counter arguments and/or connections to other topics *See the "Academic Argument" example in Chapter 8*
Systems in biology, geography, computer science, political science, etc.	1. Input 2. Output 3. Purpose or function of the system 4. Component parts and how they fit together 5. How each component part operates 6. Control of the system 7. Typical malfunctions of the system *See the "Biology" example below, p. ###*
Mathematical problems in science, engineering, and in some social sciences courses	1. Allowable key formula(s) 2. Definitions 3. Additional important information 4. Simple examples or explanations 5. List of relevant knowns and unknowns *See example of the "Concept Summary" in Chapter 7*
Literature courses	1. Genre 2. Narrative/plot 3. Setting 4. Theme 5. Characters 6. Voice 7. Tone 8. Imagery/symbolism 9. Culture/philosophy 10. Emotions 11. Style *See the "Literature Elements" in Chapter 8*

First, make sure you have a TITLE for the topic. Suppose you chose the section in your textbook entitled "Mammalian Circulatory System." This is one of five sections in a chapter on transport mechanisms.

Second, choose a list of GENERAL CATEGORIES that are appropriate to this topic. As it is a biological system, the appropriate list would be:

1. Input
2. Output
3. Purpose or function of the system
4. Component parts and how they fit together
5. How each component part operates
6. Control of the system
7. Typical malfunctions of the system

Third, use these general categories to guide your selection of SPECIFIC DETAILS for the mammalian circulatory system. Note that not all of the general categories will appear in all topics. In the example of the mammalian circulatory system, no mention is made regarding controls for the system or typical malfunctions.

Fourth, think about how you will lay out your summary of specific details in your notes. Graphic organizers can make a topic much easier to learn, because they help you to see how that information is structured. The kind of layout you choose really depends on what topics you are learning and what works best for you.[4] Some layout options to consider for memory structures are:

- a hierarchical chart
- a table
- a flowchart
- a web or mind map.

The best layout for this example, which involves a biological system, is a flowchart, as shown in Figure 6.2. The general categories and specific details of this system are shown in hierarchical form above the flowchart.

CONSOLIDATING INFORMATION IN LONG-TERM MEMORY

You have just learned the importance to memory of seeking out structure in information. However, forgetting is a fact of life, and time can erode some of what you so carefully learned. As a Good Strategy User, what can you do to consolidate information and

FIGURE 6.2   A Flowchart Illustrating Structured Information

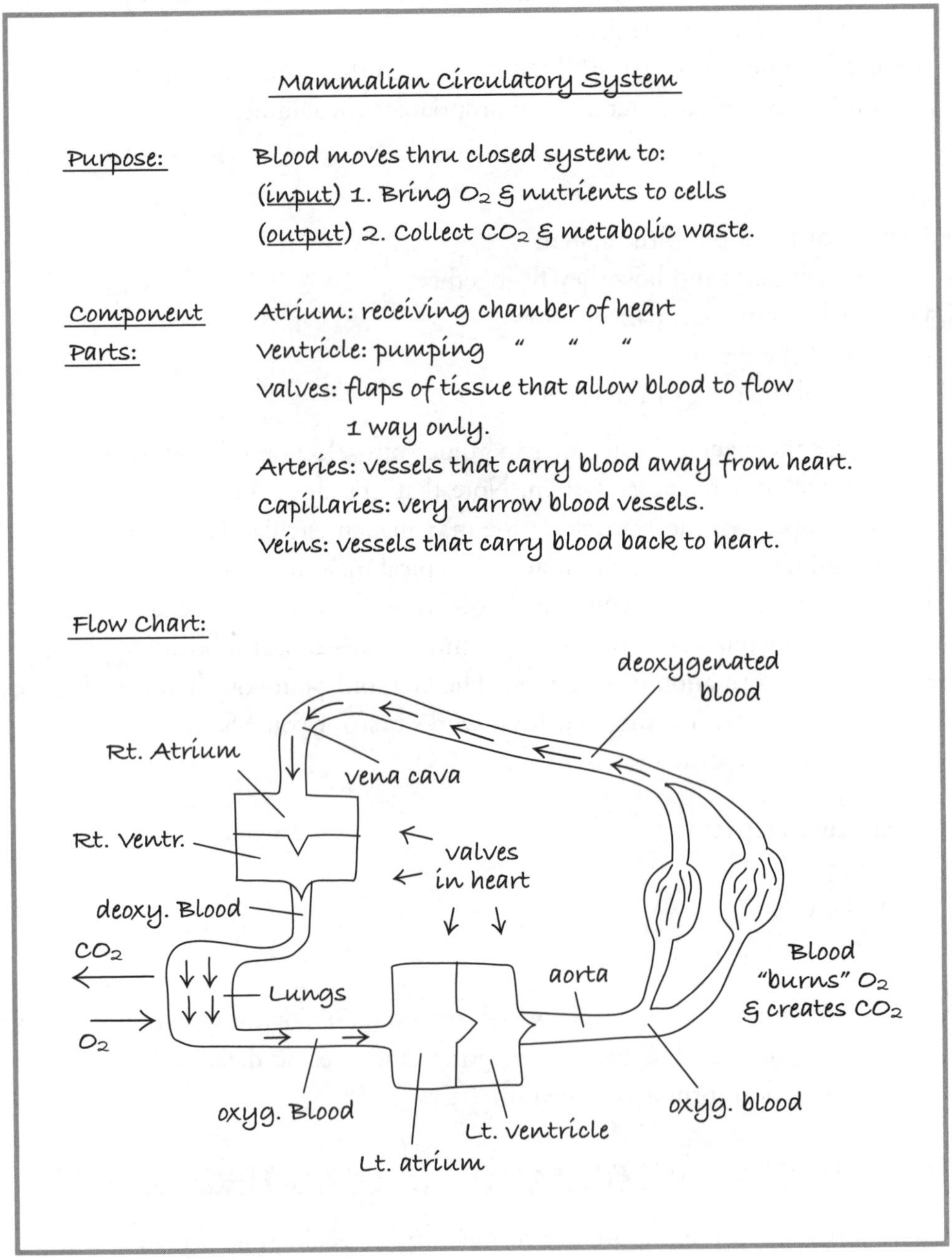

Mammalian Circulatory System

Purpose: Blood moves thru closed system to:
            (input) 1. Bring O_2 & nutrients to cells
            (output) 2. Collect CO_2 & metabolic waste.

Component   Atrium: receiving chamber of heart
Parts: Ventricle: pumping   "   "   "
              valves: flaps of tissue that allow blood to flow
                        1 way only.
              Arteries: vessels that carry blood away from heart.
              Capillaries: very narrow blood vessels.
              Veins: vessels that carry blood back to heart.

Flow Chart:

deoxygenated blood

Rt. Atrium

vena cava

Rt. Ventr.

valves in heart

deoxy. Blood

CO_2

O_2

Lungs

aorta

Blood "burns" O_2 & creates CO_2

oxyg. Blood

Lt. ventricle

oxyg. blood

Lt. atrium

thus avoid forgetting? When we forget, we mainly lose our connection to a thought, but we do not always lose the thought itself. If we want to retain as much information as possible, we have to make many connections, so that if we lose one there are still plenty of other connections to do the job. You also want to keep the information as fresh as possible and not let it slip away. You can strengthen your memory by applying two types of strategies: association strategies and review and/or rehearsal strategies.

ASSOCIATION STRATEGIES

The following association strategies will enable you to consolidate information in long-term memory. They are highlighted individually because of their unique contributions to effective storage of information, but they are often used together:

- Generate Examples
- Apply Visual Imagery
- Seek Out Connections among Ideas
- Create Mnemonics

Generate Examples

Make up your own examples and, if appropriate, counterexamples of new topics that you are learning. A counterexample is something that would *not* illustrate a concept. This is especially useful in science. In an environmental chemistry course, for example, you might think of cleaning products used in the home that are acid in composition. Counterexamples would be those products that are basic and not acidic.

Often the most powerful associations are those that relate to your own personal experiences. This is easier to do in some courses—kinesiology, geography, psychology, and sociology—than it is in others. You will tend to remember personal examples in a meaningful manner. In kinesiology, for example, when learning about muscle groups in the arm you can stretch and flex your arm to feel these individual muscles in action.

Apply Visual Imagery

Visual images are often easy to remember, so try to create an image that captures the new topic you are learning. Images can be directly related to the new topic. For example, to illustrate your understanding of operant learning in psychology, you can *visualize* your dog bounding up to you for his "positive reinforcer" (dog biscuit). Visual images can also be based on analogies that are especially important to understanding complex and abstract concepts: the simple geometric form of a pyramid can be used to describe the structure of a large business organization or government department; the flow of water in a pipe can help to explain the flow of electricity in an electronics course. An analogy acts as a model, the purpose of which is to simplify the complexity of the real world and enhance your memory of that information. The special power of visual imagery is that it enables you to transform abstract concepts into more concrete images, a well-known method for consolidating memory.

Seek Out Connections among Ideas

In any one course, make connections among ideas presented in class and information from the text, lab, or tutorial. Also, relate together information from different courses, especially courses in the same field that build on each other. At times, you may have to check back to notes from previous courses to reactivate and reinforce essential basic concepts. Unless you can get a sense of the big picture, you will not be able to understand fully the individual concepts presented. The big-picture setting is essential to a sound and flexible memory.

Create Mnemonics

Mnemonics are memory devices that involve making arbitrary, but easy to remember, associations. They might involve colour, shapes, images, or anything that can be linked to information you have to remember. Mnemonics do have one drawback: they do not involve meaningful associations, and so should be used sparingly for very specific information that you are having trouble remembering. Do you remember "Every Good Boy Deserves Fudge" from your music classes? Mnemonics such as this one can be powerful and allow you to recall detailed and complex ideas. Used appropriately, mnemonics are often essential for an optimal exam-review plan. The following are just a few of the most commonly used types:

- Rhymes
- Sounds
- Acronyms
- First Letters
- Loci

Rhymes

Rhymes are catchy and allow us to recite information that would be difficult as plain prose. If you enjoy playing with language, you might try making up some rhymes in your next test review. Rhymes do not have to be long to be effective. One student used the short and sweet mnemonic of "*Id* is the kid" to remember part of Freud's basic three-part theory about human personality.

Sounds

Simple sounds can be tied to facts that you may find hard to remember. In a biology class on genetics, for example, you will learn about the phenotype and genotype. How can you remember which is which? The sound of "fffff" can help you through association. The word phenotype begins with the "fffff" sound, as do the words "face" and "photo." These words will remind you that "(fffff)enotype" is the visible expression of the genetic makeup (i.e., what you can see), just as you can see a face or a photo.

Acronyms

Acronyms are very special words, as each letter represents something of importance to remember. The term "sohcahtoa" is an easily remembered acronym summarizing the important trigonometric definitions of sine, cosine, and tangent (sine equals opposite over hypotenuse, etc.). In physics, the colours of the spectrum can be remembered with the acronym ROY G. BIV. When you are learning your French verbs, you may come across the acronym of DR and MRS VANDERTRAMPP, representing the verbs in the past tense that are conjugated with *être* instead of with *avoir*.

First Letters

There are some types of information that are really difficult to remember without mnemonics. They might be drugs in a pharmacology class, bones and muscles in an anatomy class, or hormones in a physiology class. One way to memorize them is to generate a sentence in which the first letter of each word is the first letter of the item you have to remember (see the music example earlier). You might also recognize this mnemonic from biology: kings play chess on frosted glass surfaces, which helps you to remember the relationships among kingdom, phylum, class, order, family, genus, and species.

Loci

The Latin word *locus* means a place, so this mnemonic has to do with associating information with places. If you have a visual learning style or just enjoy visual imagery, this mnemonic can be a lot of fun to create. There are many ways to interpret the loci mnemonic. Many memory books suggest creating mental images of items that you are trying to remember and associating them with different locations in your house. A somewhat different interpretation is illustrated by the following example that uses a hand-drawn map noting seven locations to help you to remember a theory of noted psychologist Albert Ellis. He believed that the lives of many people are made difficult by irrational beliefs that they hold. Seven irrational beliefs, according to Ellis,[5] are as follows:

1. We should be Loved by absolutely everyone.
2. We should be Competent in all areas.
3. People who are Wicked should always be punished.
4. We should always try to Avoid difficulties.
5. Any Past event that was traumatic will always haunt us.
6. If things are Not the way we want them to be, then life is a disaster.
7. Problems that we face are Externally caused.

To use the loci mnemonic, for each irrational belief one word has been chosen as being able to encapsulate the idea, and the first letter has been capitalized. In Figure 6.3, a map of a familiar area was quickly hand drawn (in this case, southwestern Ontario). Seven locations were chosen that began with those seven first letters, and the place names have been placed on the map. The visual impact of the map allows relatively easy recall of those seven places. For the mnemonic to work well for you, choose an area that you know well. Enough memory work needs to be done to connect those seven letters to the seven ideas.

REVIEW AND/OR REHEARSAL STRATEGIES

Rehearsal strategies are extremely important for consolidating information in long-term memory because they give you practice doing what you will be doing on a test—

FIGURE 6.3   An Application of the Loci Mnemonic

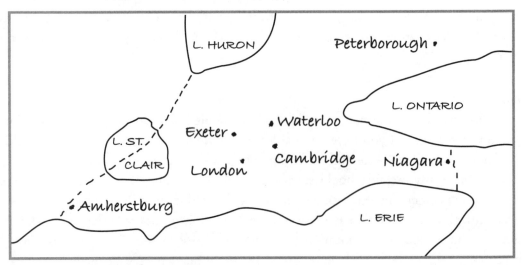

retrieving information from long-term memory. In the time period immediately before a test, most of your study time should be spent using these rehearsal strategies:

- Recite Key Ideas
- Predict Questions
- Review Old Exams

Recite Key Ideas

Using headings or titles as cues, try to recall the specific details under each heading you have learned. This procedure is both simple and portable—you can do it almost anywhere (e.g., sitting on a bus or while washing the dishes). Also, if you have the opportunity, you might get other people involved by giving them your study notes and asking them to check how well you remember the content. Recitation trains your retrieval processes and is especially important in preparing for multiple-choice exams, where you need a reliable memory of many concepts. For problem-solving and essay exams, some recitation is necessary but you must also balance it with the application of ideas.

Predict Questions

In all courses, spend time predicting likely test questions for each topic. This can be done in a variety of ways:

- Keep your memory structures in mind and generate questions around specific details from your lecture notes and texts.
- Check out questions that are posed in your text or study guide.
- Look through homework questions that you were assigned and think how you could adapt them for the test.
- Share questions with others.

Review Old Exams

If available, old exams provide you with excellent opportunities to rehearse writing real exams. As far as possible, simulate exam conditions by working in a quiet and undisturbed location. Avoid falling into the trap of looking up the answer right after trying a question, especially if you are having difficulty retrieving information from long-term memory. Before checking with your textbook or looking up the answer, give yourself time to activate a variety of retrieval cues. You may find that the required information will suddenly flash back into your short-term memory. This struggle to remember is good training for the real exam.

THE CRUCIAL ROLE OF COMPREHENSION MONITORING

As powerful as the ideas and strategies presented in this chapter are, their effectiveness hinges on a crucial factor—your ability to monitor your comprehension. If you do not understand something, you will probably not remember it; and even if you do manage to memorize the information, you will likely have difficulty in applying it to new situations. Box 6.1 is a checklist of symptoms that might indicate a comprehension problem. Use it to monitor your comprehension for one of your courses, and feel free to add, in the extra spaces, any other symptoms that you may be experiencing.

BOX 6.1   Comprehension Monitoring

NAME OF COURSE: _____

Cognitive Symptoms of Comprehension Problems

_____   1. In class, everything moves too fast for me.

_____   2. There are so many details that I can't see any big picture.

_____   3. I can't generate any examples on my own.

_____   4. Even though I study a lot, I can't remember very much of this stuff.

_____   5. I find it difficult to focus my attention when trying to learn this material.

_____   6. This topic just doesn't make sense to me.

7. _____

8. _____

Emotional Symptoms of Comprehension Problems

_____   1. I have this gut feeling that I haven't really grasped this topic yet.

_____   2. I feel overwhelmed, even scared, by the information.

_____   3. I feel angry about having to learn this junk.

_____   4. This stuff is so boring.

_____   5. I am not at all confident of my ability to do this task.

_____   6. I wish I were not taking this course.

7. _____

8. _____

PUTTING THESE IDEAS TO WORK

This chapter began by introducing a model of memory systems. In particular, it encouraged you to think about the challenge presented to you by each one of the model's three components. The major contribution of this chapter, though, is to emphasize the importance of creating memory structures as you learn. Establishing a soundly structured memory is a key goal to aim for, and once you have created a memory, you need to maintain it. Forgetting will happen, but your reinforcement of memories can maintain them longer and re-create them faster.

Your challenge at this point is to put these ideas into practice. It does not have to involve a drastic change to the way that you do things. Developing more effective study strategies can be done one small step at a time. However, powerful thinking strategies can make a real difference to your learning. These ideas will be reinforced as you read the next two chapters, "Focus on Problem Solving and Labs" and "Focus on the Social Sciences and Humanities."

WEB ALERT!

The University of Western Ontario
London, Ontario
www.sdc.uwo.ca/learning/paths.html?topics
Click on the links for "Effective Memory Strategies" and "Structuring Information."

Middle Tennessee State University
Murfreesboro, Tennessee
www.mtsu.edu/~studskl/mem.html
Memory Principles.

University of Waterloo
Waterloo, Ontario
www.adm.uwaterloo.ca/infocs/study_skills/learning.html
Study Skills: Learning and Remembering.

CHAPTER ENDNOTES

1. Atkinson, R. C., & Shiffrin, R. M. (1968). Human memory: A proposed system and its control processes. In K. W. Spence (Ed.), *The psychology of learning and motivation: Advances in research and theory* (pp. 89–195). New York: Academic Press.

2. Mestre, R., & Touger, J. (1989). Cognitive research—What's in it for physics teachers? *The Physics Teacher, 23,* 447–456.

3. Bransford, J. D., & Johnson, M. K. (1992). Contextual prerequisites for understanding: Some investigations of comprehension and recall. *Journal of Verbal Learning and Verbal Behavior, 11,* 717–26.

4. See more on graphic organizers in Chapter 4, "Learning from Lectures."

5. Ellis, A. (1967). Rational-emotive psychotherapy. In D. Arbuckle (ed.), *Counseling and psychotherapy: An existential-humanistic view.* New York: McGraw-Hill.

Chapter 7

FOCUS ON PROBLEM SOLVING AND LABS

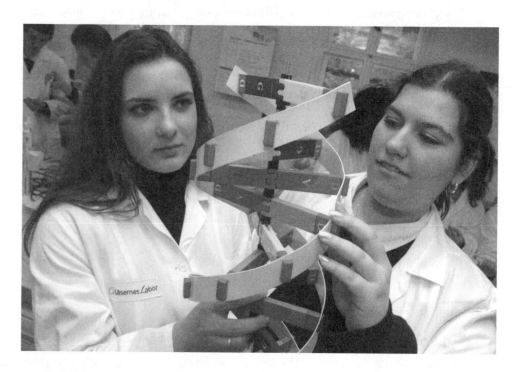

LEARNING OBJECTIVES

The purpose of this chapter is for you to:

- Learn how to solve problems efficiently.
- Learn how to make better use of the resources and study time available to you.
- Learn strategies for understanding concepts quickly and solving problems confidently.
- Learn strategies for the efficient and successful completion of laboratory work.

Have you ever wondered why some students do well in problem-solving courses such as math, physics, and statistics, while others do poorly? Natural ability accounts for some of this difference, but the strategies that students use are also very important in successful problem-solving performance. To be a Good Strategy User when it comes to mathematical problem solving, you need to keep in mind the two different kinds of strategies introduced in Chapter 1, "The Good Strategy User":

1. Self-management strategies that deal with issues such as how you manage your time and your use of resources.
2. Thinking strategies that deal with how you structure and use information.

This chapter explores both kinds of strategies as they apply to problem-solving courses and labs.

MANAGING YOUR PROBLEM-SOLVING ACTIVITIES

In order to manage your problem-solving activities effectively, you need to do the following:

- Work on Your Problem-Solving Courses Regularly
- Choose Problems Wisely
- Solve Problems on Your Own
- Set a Time Limit
- Develop Useful Help Resources
- Do Some Uncalculated Solutions
- Have the Necessary Background and Skills
- Keep Your Attitude Positive

WORK ON YOUR PROBLEM-SOLVING COURSES REGULARLY

Schedule regular periods in the week for working on each of your problem-solving courses. This is very important for two reasons:

1. Problem-solving courses are often sequential, and so understanding today's concept often depends on knowing last week's material.
2. At times, you will need help in learning about concepts and their application, and this can't be done at the last minute just before a test.

CHOOSE PROBLEMS WISELY

You do not have to solve all the practice problems. Many students waste a considerable amount of time and energy slavishly trying to solve every practice problem available. Some students do this because they believe that they will learn how to solve each and every possible problem, while others believe that "more is always better." Remember that your goal in doing practice problems is to learn how to apply a given concept to solve a variety of relevant problems. Usually, there are only a few significantly different kinds of difficult problems associated with a given concept. (See "Range of Problems Strategy" on page 117.) Therefore, choose a few easy problems first to see if you can apply the concept confidently. Then look for appropriate problems that are difficult in significantly different ways, and do only as many of those as you need to feel fairly confident. For example, most math, chemistry, and physics texts have at least 50 practice problems associated with a single concept, usually in increasing order of difficulty. By choosing wisely, you might have to do only 15 to 20 of those 50 problems to gain the confidence needed to apply the concept correctly to any possible exam question.

Solve Problems on Your Own

Many students avoid getting down to solving problems by spending too much time rereading the text and lecture notes or looking at examples of solved problems. Because exams in these courses require that you solve problems on your own, you need to practise doing just that. Therefore, you should try to learn the basics of each concept as quickly as possible, and then get right into trying to solve the relevant problems. This also means concentrating on learning the basics in the lecture (as opposed to just taking notes) so that you can minimize the time you have to spend reading over the ideas after class. Once you understand the basic concepts, re-solve the solved examples in both the text and the lecture, and then start the new practice problems.

Set a Time Limit

Many students get stuck when trying to solve a problem and can spend an hour or two making little progress. Unfortunately, if you do run across a few problems like this, you can expend a lot of study time and have very little, other than frustration, to show for it. This "getting-stuck" pattern is certainly a major factor in the failure of many students in problem-solving courses. So, plan to attempt at least four problems in one hour. Use a timer if necessary, and after the first 15 minutes go on to the next problem even if you are stuck on the first one. What do you do about the problems you cannot solve? The next strategy suggests some ways to get "unstuck."

Develop Useful Help Resources

When stuck on a problem, most students typically consult their lecture notes and text, but sometimes these resources do not help. However, there are other help resources such as your instructor, tutorial assistant, the help centre, tutors, other students (small groups of two to four students working on problems together), different texts, and problem solution books (e.g., the *Schaum's Outlines* series, a resource containing many worked examples of problems for courses in math, physics, economics, and other problem-based disciplines). The Internet also has sites that display solved problems in a variety of courses. Good Strategy Users often use a greater range of help resources than do less successful students. However, to use resources effectively, you need to identify your specific difficulties as concisely as you can and, of course, you actually have to go for help.

Do Some Uncalculated Solutions

You may not have to solve every practice problem completely. In an uncalculated solution, you only set up the solution, but you do not actually carry out the arithmetic or algebraic calculations to get the final answer. Because the complete solution to many problems requires considerable calculation, you can save considerable study time by setting up an uncalculated solution for every second or third problem you tackle. However, you should use this strategy only if you have first successfully and completely solved a few problems with the new concept and if your arithmetic or algebraic skills do not need improvement through practice.

Have the Necessary Background and Skills

Because problem-solving courses such as statistics and physics are required courses for certain programs or degrees, there is a great temptation to attempt these courses without having the adequate background knowledge and skills. This can make a difficult course just about impossible. To avoid this trap, make an early investigation into any problem-solving courses you need to take. Talk to the instructor, get a course outline or old exam, and see what kind of background is really necessary. If your background is weak, there are ways you can remedy that. Many institutions have specialized learning centres that offer diagnostic testing and self-paced instruction. Also, distance education courses are available in a variety of subjects. If your weaknesses are not so serious, you could strengthen your knowledge and skills by working through an appropriate text on your own.

Keep Your Attitude Positive

It is all too common to hear statements from unsuccessful students such as: *"I hate calculus. There are so many formulas to memorize in physics. You have to be a nerd to really get that stuff."* Negative attitudes such as these can be very damaging to your effectiveness as a learner in a problem-solving course. Monitor what you are saying to yourself or to others about the problem-solving courses you are taking. If negative attitudes and beliefs are creeping in, try replacing them with more positive but realistic self-talk such as: *"If I work on understanding this stuff, I can get it. There's got to be a fairly simple idea underneath all this. I must be missing something because I know it's not meant to be so difficult."* You might try asking a few successful students how they view the course and evaluate how their comments compare to your own. Try to foster a positive attitude to the courses you take.

THREE KEY THINKING STRATEGIES

Educational research indicates that there are very real differences in the ways in which successful and unsuccessful students approach the solving of problems.[1] As discussed in Chapter 6, unsuccessful students favour an unstructured, formula-memorizing approach, while successful students opt for an information-structuring or conceptual approach. In other words, unsuccessful students memorize many specific formulas and solutions, and then try to match them to the problem at hand. However, Good Strategy Users learn how to apply a few key formulas and a small amount of important conceptual information to many different situations. Fortunately, research also shows that students can become more successful problem-solvers by learning to use this conceptual approach.[2]

The conceptual approach to science problem solving involves three separate but interconnected learning goals as shown below. To achieve each of these goals, a specific learning strategy is recommended, and is identified in brackets after the goal:

GOAL #1   To learn and understand the small amount of information essential to each concept. *(Concept Summary Strategy)*

GOAL #2   To apply this small amount of conceptual information to solve actual problems. *(Decision Steps Strategy)*

GOAL #3   To anticipate and prepare for the more difficult problems that often appear on exams. *(Range of Problems Strategy)*

CONCEPT SUMMARY STRATEGY

As in other types of courses, creating efficient memory structures is crucial to selecting and learning the key information in problem-solving courses. The concept summary strategy guides you as you create a memory structure for each important concept you encounter. Recall from Chapter 6 that efficient memory structures involve organizing information on three different levels: the title, general categories, and specific details. So in the concept summary strategy, you first identify the title of the concept, then you use a checklist of general categories (suited to problem-solving courses) to select specific details.

Identify the Title of the Concept

You can find the titles of concepts in the course outline or in your textbook's table of contents. Typically, one concept involves a few very powerful general ideas that are usually expressed as key formulas. The mole in chemistry, the limit of a function in mathematics, the t-test in statistics, and Newton's second law in physics would all be examples of concepts. However, determining a single concept in a lecture or chapter can be a little tricky at first, so look for how the practice problems are organized. Sometimes each heading in a chapter has problems related specifically to it. This often occurs in math courses where there are a number of smaller and distinct concepts in each chapter. However, in other courses like physics and chemistry, a chapter may present only one or two large concepts that are subdivided into smaller but related concepts for ease of explanation. Then, it is better to group the smaller concepts of the chapter into one larger concept. For example, the concepts of acid, base, and pH can be grouped together as one concept rather than as three related concepts.

Use Categories to Select and Learn the Specific Details

Here are the general categories for problem-solving courses:

- Allowable Key Formula(s)
- Definitions
- Additional Important Information
- Simple Examples or Explanations
- List of Relevant Knowns and Unknowns

Allowable Key Formula(s)

Usually, a specific concept consists of one or a few key formulas that you are allowed to use. All other related formulas are special cases that can readily be derived from first principles, so these related formulas need not be memorized. If you have trouble identifying which formulas are the key ones, ask the instructor or look on the summary page of the text.

Definitions

To apply a key formula correctly, you need to know what each term in the formula means. Therefore, you need to define every new term you come across, including units and symbols.

Additional Important Information

This is information you need so that you can apply the formulas correctly: sign conventions, special characteristics of terms, reference values, the meaning of zero values, and situations in which the key formulas do not work. For example, the slope of a line is positive if the line slopes upward, negative if the line slopes downward, and zero if the line is flat.

Simple Examples or Explanations

By providing simple examples or explanations in your own words, diagrams, or analogies, you can test your level of understanding. Expressing the basics of a concept in different ways forces you to think more deeply about the concept. Often, just thinking about a simple example or analogy and sketching a diagram of the concept at work can be very helpful in this regard.

List of Relevant Knowns and Unknowns

When faced with a variety of problems to solve, many students find it difficult to know which concept applies to which problem. To avoid this difficulty, list the crucial knowns and unknowns (and their common synonyms) that need to be presented in a problem in order to signal to you that this particular concept should be applied. For example, problems in Newton's second law and problems in kinematics may both ask for, or give, the acceleration of an object. However, problems in Newton's second law also include mass and force, while those in kinematics involve velocities and time.

For the next concept you encounter try making a concept summary of the specific details on a sheet of paper or on a 5 x 8 card (see Figure 7.1). Do this before you attempt any problems related to that concept. When you do start tackling the problems, be sure to review this concept summary sheet first, and then keep it handy for reference.

FIGURE 7.1   An Example of a Concept Summary

<u>Concept</u>: Straight-line Kinematics: Constant Acceleration

<u>Allowable Key Formulas</u>:

1. $\vec{v}_f = \vec{v}_i + \vec{a}\,(\Delta t)$ 2. $\vec{x}_f = \vec{x}_i + \vec{v}_i\,(\Delta t) + \frac{1}{2}\vec{a}\,(\Delta t)^2$

3. $\vec{v}_f^{\,2} = \vec{v}_i^{\,2} + 2\vec{a}\,(\Delta \vec{x})$

<u>Definitions</u>:

$\vec{v}_i$ and $\vec{v}_f$ are initial and final velocities of object in m/s

$\vec{a}$ is acceleration of object in m/s^2

$\vec{x}_i$ and $\vec{x}_f$ are initial and final positions of object in m

Δt is time taken for object to move from $\vec{x}_i$ to $\vec{x}_f$ in s

(continued)

(continued)

Additional Important Information:

1. $\vec{x}$, $\vec{v}$, $\vec{a}$ are <u>vector</u> quantities. ∴ choose a + direction in a problem

   and be consistent.

2. $g = 9.8$ m/s² downward.

3. When $\vec{a} = 0$ object moves with constant velocity.

4. These formulas <u>only</u> work for one value of constant acceleration.

Explanation:

These formulas relate <u>2</u> points on path of object undergoing constant acceleration

List of Relevant Knowns and Unknowns:

Use these formulas with problems (or parts of) that involve:

1. "acceleration" or "speeding up," "slowing down," "braking,"

   "coming to rest"

2. "velocities" or "speeds"—assuming direction is known

3. "positions," "displacements," or distances (assumed direction)

4. "time" taken for object to move between 2 points

DECISION STEPS STRATEGY

To solve problems well you need to make accurate decisions about how a given concept applies to a specific situation. In a lecture it can be easy to follow the instructor's accurate decisions about how to apply a specific concept to a problem, but when you are faced with a new problem to solve on your own, it is often difficult to know where to start—that is, what decision is first? If you are like many students, you may try to handle this situation by either plugging numbers into formulas blindly or by trying to memorize every solution you can. Neither of these approaches works very well. A better approach is to keep track of the decision steps you need to follow in order to solve problems logically from first principles (i.e., concept summary).

Decision steps focus on the key decisions that lead to the correct application of a concept instead of focusing on the computations that are actually the result of applying good decision steps. Frequently in lectures instructors will state the decision steps they are following, but they do not usually write these decision steps down. As a result, many students focus on the mathematical equations and computations that are written down and not on the decision steps that generated them. Therefore, for some problems try to record decision steps in words in your lecture notes as well as in mathematical notation. After class you may want to revise and record them more neatly beside one or two of the solved examples (as shown in Figures 7.2, 7.3, and 7.4). Therefore, the decision steps strategy involves the following:

- Analyze Solved Examples to Get Decision Steps
- Use and Revise Your Decision Steps

Analyze Solved Examples to Get Decision Steps

The steps of correctly solved examples should be carefully analyzed by answering one or more of these questions for each step:

- What was done in this step?
- How was it done (i.e., which formula or guideline was used)?
- Why was it done?

Good decision steps can clarify basic problem-solving tasks for specific concepts by identifying knowns and unknowns and applying formulas as needed. To be most useful, each decision step should be quite brief and focus on a step you find tricky.

Use and Revise Your Decision Steps

After you have written down a few decision steps based on the analysis of a solved example, try to "test run" these steps on a similar problem. Usually, your initial decision steps are imperfect and incomplete, so revision is needed.

RANGE OF PROBLEMS STRATEGY

The practice problems in a textbook associated with a specific concept usually start with quite easy problems and then increase in difficulty. Unfortunately, it is often the more difficult problems that show up on the test. Usually, there are only a few significantly

FIGURE 7.2   Decision Steps Applied to a Solved Physics Problem

Problem

A police car begins accelerating from rest at 2.0 m/s^2 in pursuit of a pair of bank robbers who are travelling in a getaway car at a constant velocity of 20 m/s. If the police were originally 100 m behind when they started, when and where will they catch the bank robbers?

Steps	Solution

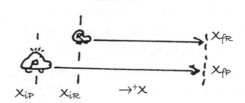

1. Diagram initial and final positions of each body.

   origin →

   X_{iP} X_{iR} →$+X$

2. Choose +X direction and origin.

3. Make a table identifying initial and final values for each body.
   Note:
   - Watch signs!
   - X_i's depend on origin.

   Police
   $V_i = 0$
   $a = +2 m/s^2$
   $X_{iP} = 0$
   $X_{fP} = ?$ ← *same* →
   $\Delta t = ?$ ← " →

   Robbers
   $V_{iR} = V_{fR} = +20 m/s$
   $a = 0$
   $X_{iR} = +100m$
   $X_{fR} = ?$
   $\Delta t = ?$

4. Apply this formula to each body:
   $X_f = X_i + V_i(\Delta t) + \frac{1}{2}a(\Delta t)^2$
   (i.e., produce 2 equations)

   $X_{fP} = 0 + 0 + \frac{1}{2}(2)(\Delta t)^2 = (\Delta t)^2$

   $X_{fR} = 100 + 20(\Delta t)$

5. Relate these 2 equations.
   (usually they are equal)

   $\therefore (\Delta t)^2 = 100 + 20(\Delta t)$

   $\to \Delta t = 24.1s$ (by quadratic)

6. Solve and check answers to see if X_f's are equal.
   (note: report answer noting your origin)

   $\therefore X_{fP} = 581m$
   $\& X_{fR} = 582m$ } ok

   from where police started

FIGURE 7.3   Decision Steps for Acid–Base Problems in Chemistry[3]

Problem

Find the pH of a solution prepared by adding 300 mL of 0.100 M acetic acid and 200 mL of 0.100 M NaOH. (K_a of acetic acid is 1.85×10^{-5})

Steps	Solution

1. Identify each species in problem.

    4 possibilities:

    a) strong acid or base → know these!

    b) weak acid or base → not strong!

    c) conjugate acid or base

    d) spectator salt

2. Is there an acid-base reaction?

    (except weak and its conjugate)

    If No → go to step 3

    If Yes:

    a) Write acid/base reaction (with no back reaction!)

    b) Do stoichiometry on this reaction to find what's left.

3. Identify what's left.

    4 possibilities:

    a) If weak & conjugate left → use buffer equation (moles or concentration).

    b) If conjugate only left →
   - find its concentration
   - set up equil. equation for conj. + H_2O weak + OH^- or H_3O^+
   - $K_w = K_a K_b$ ⇌

    c) If strong only → find pH by simply finding OH^- or H_3O^+ concentration of strong.

    d) If strong only → find other ion concentration use common ion.

Solution

• acetic acid (HAc) → <u>weak</u> acid

• $NaOH$ → <u>strong</u> base

∴ <u>there is acid-base reaction</u>

    $HAc = (0.300 L)(0.100 M)$

        $= 0.030$ moles

§ $OH^- = 0.020$ moles

∴ $HAc + OH^- \rightarrow Ac^- + H_2O$

I: 0.030   0.020   ∅

R: $\underline{-0.020}$ $\underline{-0.020}$ $\underline{+0.020}$
F: 0.010   ∅   0.020

∴ weak & conjugate left

           ↙

    is buffer (possibility a)

    [I can use moles]

∴ $HAc + H_2O \rightleftharpoons Ac^- + H_3O^+$

E: 0.010   0.020   x

Set up Ka:

→ $1.85 \times 10^{-5} = \dfrac{(0.020)(x)}{0.010}$

→ $x = 9.25 \times 10^{-6} M$

∴ pH $= 5.03$

FIGURE 7.4   Decision Steps for Related Rates in Calculus[4]

1. Sketch a diagram of the situation and show given values

2. Identify variables needed to specify the known and unknown rates:
   - 'anchor' lengths of variables on diagram
   - use derivative (with respect to time) notation of variables for rates

3. Find a mathematical relationship between these variables:
   - from geometry (unless relationship is given)
   - common possibilities:
     - Pythagoras
     - Similar triangles
     - Volume formulas: cones, tanks, spheres...
     - Volume formulas + Pythagoras or similar triangles

4. Simplify this relationship

5. Differentiate both sides of the relationship with respect to time

6. Substitute in the given values

7. Solve for unknown rate

Problem: Pat, the math teacher, has just finished a night class and is walking in a straight line away from the math building at a rate of 1.5 m/s. There is a light at the entrance to the building that is 4.5 m above the ground. If Pat is 1.8 m in height, how fast is her shadow lengthening?

Solution:

① 4.5 m, 1.8 m, y, x

② Let x = length of shadow from Pat's feet
y = Pat's distance from bldg.

$$\therefore \frac{dy}{dt} = 1.5 \text{ m/s}; \quad \frac{dx}{dt} = ?$$

③ By similar triangles:

$$\frac{x}{1.8} = \frac{x + y}{4.5}$$

④ $\longrightarrow 4.5x = 1.8x + 1.8y$

$\longrightarrow 2.7x = 1.8y$

⑤ Differentiate w.r.t time $\quad 2.7\dfrac{dx}{dt} = 1.8\dfrac{dy}{dt}$

⑥ & ⑦ and $\dfrac{dx}{dt} = \dfrac{1.8}{2.7}(1.5 \text{ m/s}) = 1.0 \text{ m/s}$

different types of difficult problems associated with a given concept. The majority of practice problems are just minor variations of one of these types. This strategy of identifying the range of problems helps you to identify some of the common types of difficult problems associated with a specific concept. The intention in doing this is to change your perspective from that of a passive receiver who hopes for easy problems but often receives difficult ones to that of a strategist who can effectively anticipate and solve the full range of problems from the easiest to the most difficult. For a Good Strategy User, the range of problems strategy involves the following:

- Know the Common Kinds of Difficult Problems
- Anticipate the Different Kinds of Difficult Problems
- List the Range of Problems from Easy to Difficult

Know the Common Kinds of Difficult Problems
Here are most of the common kinds of difficult problems (feel free to add others):

- **Hidden knowns:** Needed information is hidden in a phrase or diagram (e.g., "at rest" means $v = 0$).
- **Multipart—same concept:** A problem may comprise two or more subproblems, each involving the use of the same concept. This type of problem can be solved only by identifying the given information in the light of these subproblems.
- **Multipart—different concepts:** Same idea as above, except now the subproblems involve the use of different concepts.
- **Multipart—simultaneous equations:** Same idea as above, except no one subproblem can be solved fully by itself. You may have two unknowns and two equations or three unknowns and three equations, and you will have to solve them simultaneously (e.g., through substitution, comparison, addition and subtraction, or matrices, etc.).
- **Work backward:** Some problems look difficult because to solve them you have to work in reverse order from problems that you have previously solved.
- **Letters only:** When known quantities are expressed in letters, problems can look difficult, but if you follow the decision steps, these are not usually so difficult.
- **"Dummy" variables:** Sometimes a quantity that you feel should be a known is not specified because it is not really needed—that is, it cancels out (e.g., mass in work-energy problems, temperature in gas-law problems).
- **Red herrings (extra information):** A problem may give you more information than you need. This can be unnerving if you expect to use all of the given information.

Anticipate the Different Kinds of Difficult Problems

As you attempt the practice problems associated with a specific concept, anticipate that different kinds of difficult problems should be arising, and be ready to solve them. Typically, then, the first few problems associated with a new concept will be fairly straightforward applications of the key formula(s). As you progress through the problems, though, you will start to see some that need to be worked backward, others with hidden knowns, two- and three-part problems, and so on.

List the Range of Problems from Easy to Difficult

After you have finished studying a specific concept, make a list of the range of problem types from easy to difficult that you encountered as well as any other difficult types that are likely and "testable." Include a brief reference to a specific example for each type of difficult problem you identify. (See Figure 7.5.)

SUCCESS IN THE LAB

Many problem-solving courses require a few hours working in the lab each week and often more hours at home completing the lab report. This lab component can be worth a significant portion of the final grade, and it focuses on hands-on learning that is quite different from the conceptual learning that occurs in lectures. To handle this practical learning situation effectively, you need to apply the following relevant learning strategies:

- Find Connections between the Labs and the Course Material
- Determine How Much Each Lab Report Is Worth
- Prepare Effectively for Each Lab
- Use Your Lab Time Wisely
- Get Lab Reports Done Quickly
- Deal Quickly with Any Difficulties

FIND CONNECTIONS BETWEEN THE LABS AND THE COURSE MATERIAL

The lab component gives students a very different and practical way of experiencing the concepts and ideas taught in lectures. Sometimes the connection between lab and lecture is obvious, but sometimes students mistakenly feel that the two are almost totally separate entities. Whenever you are working on a lab, give some thought to the connections between it and the relevant course material. For example, you will often be asked to show that a particular theory or law can adequately explain the behaviour of a specific system you measure in the lab. Make sure you know the theory or law before going

FIGURE 7.5   An Example of a Range of Problems

> ⟨ STRAIGHT-LINE KINEMATICS—CONST. ACCEL ⟩
>
> I. 1-Body problems:
>   a. 1 part (i.e. 1 pair of initial & final pts.)
>   1. "Simple"-no change in direction
>   e.g. cyclist accelerates.
>   2. "Change direction"-esp up/down
>   e.g. ball goes up & down.
>
>   b. 2 or more parts (i.e. more than 1 pair of initial
>   and final pts.).
>   1. one acceleration: pts A→B, B→C, etc...
>   e.g. rock falls ½ height of cliff in last second...
>   how high is cliff?
>   2. two or more accelerations: e.g. train speeds up,
>   slows down, constant velocity, comes to stop.
>
>   c. Find Average Velocity (v_arg): for problems above
>
>
> II. 2-Body problems:
>   a. Simultaneous equations required:
>   1. Initial x's are different, e.g. police & robbers
>   2. Initial t's are different, e.g. coconuts off cliff.

Explanation

The student here has classified all the problems she has seen that are associated with this concept into "subtypes" that identify important differences
in the structure and difficulty of the problems. Note that many subtypes
are specific examples of the ways to make problems difficult. The student
has also included key words about specific examples that typify that sub-
type, e.g., cyclist problems.

to the lab, and keep it in mind as you work on the lab. By using this strategy, you take advantage of the memory principle of association, which can help your learning both in the lab and in the lecture.

DETERMINE HOW MUCH EACH LAB REPORT IS WORTH

Many students make the mistake of working far too many hours when trying to write the perfect lab report. It is essential that you spend only as much time on each lab as it is worth. Usually, the lab component is worth from 15 to 40 percent of your overall final grade, so that with five to ten lab reports due, the value of a single lab report varies from about 2 to 8 percent of your final grade. Therefore, you should plan to spend no more than two to eight hours on the report. Remember that term tests and quizzes are often worth much more than lab reports and thus merit more of your study time.

PREPARE EFFECTIVELY FOR EACH LAB

Read over the description of each lab in the lab manual shortly before you go to the actual lab session. Often, these descriptions appear to be quite complex initially, but you can simplify your preparation if you look for the following common features of most lab descriptions and find the important details that usually accompany them (you can consider this to be the lab structure):

- **Introduction:** Purpose of the lab and introduction of the relevant concepts or theories.
- **Method:** Equipment and procedure you will use to achieve the purpose (also note any special safety precautions).
- **Results:** The observations, data, diagrams, graphs, or products that you will produce in the lab. Do you need to make any data tables, diagrams, or sample calculations before going to the lab?
- **Conclusion:** The analysis and presentation of your lab results in the lab report.

USE YOUR LAB TIME WISELY

There are always a few students who manage to work through the lab more quickly and effectively than the rest of the class. Listed below are some of the strategies they use to get the most out of their lab time. Use this list to check both which of these you are currently using and which ones you should be using.

_____	Prepare well.
_____	Make a real effort to understand the purpose of the lab and connect it to the information presented in lectures.

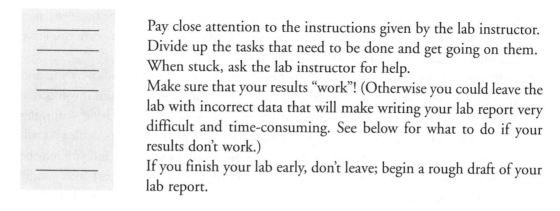

Pay close attention to the instructions given by the lab instructor.

Divide up the tasks that need to be done and get going on them.

When stuck, ask the lab instructor for help.

Make sure that your results "work"! (Otherwise you could leave the lab with incorrect data that will make writing your lab report very difficult and time-consuming. See below for what to do if your results don't work.)

If you finish your lab early, don't leave; begin a rough draft of your lab report.

GET LAB REPORTS DONE QUICKLY

If you have been using a number of the lab strategies described above, the actual writing of the report should not be very difficult or time-consuming. However, there are still some things you can do at this stage:

1. Make sure you know what the lab instructor expects to see in a good lab report. Usually you will be given guidelines on how to write the report, but, if possible, it is better to see an actual model lab report. Often the lab instructor will make a model report available.

2. Use a computer or a programmable calculator to save time whenever possible. This includes using a spreadsheet program to do repetitive calculations and produce any resulting graphics quickly. If you don't know how to use a spreadsheet program, learn! Mastering the basic operations of such a program does not take long and will save you a lot of calculation and graphing time. Also, use a word processor to write the report. You might even consider using a graphics program for specialized diagrams.

3. Third, avoid the temptation to make the lab report perfect. If you have adequately covered each of the main features expected in a good report, then stop working.

DEAL QUICKLY WITH ANY DIFFICULTIES

Even if you use all of the above strategies, there are two common challenges that you are likely to face when you are in a lab situation:

1. **Your results do not work:** Occasionally your results will not correspond with the theoretical or anticipated results. *While you are still in the lab,* ask the lab instructor to help you diagnose what went wrong. The usual reasons for this include the following: you did not follow proper procedure; you read or processed the data incor-

rectly; or your equipment malfunctioned. Once you have diagnosed the problem, you can usually redo the experiment or rework the data quite quickly. Make sure you leave the lab with data or observations that will work.

2. **Difficulty working with your partner:** There can be a variety of reasons why you and your partner do not work well together, but the most common complaint involves one of the partners having to do most of the work while the other does very little. Assuming you are a Good Strategy User and have prepared adequately, it is quite possible you will encounter a partner who does very little work. This is a tricky situation and you may be tempted to just let it pass. That's not a good idea because you will become increasingly frustrated at having to do more and more extra work. Instead, talk to your partner as soon as possible. Find out what he or she finds difficult about the lab situation. Also make your expectations about the lab work clear to your partner. Often you can find ways to take advantage of each other's strengths and encourage good teamwork. If that does not succeed, talk to your lab demonstrator or course instructor. They need to know early in the term that you are having problems with your partner. That way they can help both of you find some way to resolve the problem. Instructors are not sympathetic to students who complain about this issue at the end of term.

THE DAY-BY-DAY PROBLEM-SOLVER

Box 7.1 demonstrates how a Good Strategy User enrolled in a problem-solving course would use many of the strategies described in this chapter on a day-to-day basis. You can use this as a summary and checklist of the strategies in this chapter.

BOX 7.1   Problem-Solving Checklist

Just Before Lecture

☑ Maintain a positive attitude by remembering that a concept actually has very little information (but that information must be learned well).

During Lecture

☑ Go into class intending to learn as much as possible in the lecture. Watch for components of the concept summary.

☑ Focus on decision steps whenever an example is solved.

After Lecture (for 15 to 30 minutes)

☑ Fill in the review column of your lecture notes.

☑ Again track components of the concept summary (especially key formulas).

☑ Carefully analyze any solved examples to identify decision steps.

☑ If in doubt, refer to the text.

During That Same Week

☑ Make the concept summary.

☑ Learn components of this concept summary well.

☑ Write initial decision steps beside or near a solved example.

☑ Re-solve other lecture examples on your own by following these decision steps.

☑ Start solving practice problems by choosing a few easy, then some medium, and then some difficult ones.

☑ Always use your decision steps to solve practice problems.

☑ Revise your decision steps as you work through a variety of problems.

☑ Anticipate common kinds of difficult problems.

☑ Limit the time you spend on each problem you attempt.

☑ Maintain a positive attitude—problems are not meant to be that difficult.

☑ If stuck, get help promptly.

For Labs

☑ Use preparation and in-lab strategies.

☑ Spend only a reasonable time on the lab report.

Before Exams

☑ List the range of problems for each concept to be tested.

☑ Practise solving problems out of context by using old tests or sheets of review problems. You can also put individual problems on slips of paper, mix them in a jar, and then select a problem to be solved. The same effect can be achieved by typing problems into a computer and then randomly selecting ones to be solved.

STRATEGIES CAN MAKE THE DIFFERENCE

Problem-solving courses and the labs that often accompany them can be challenging to many students. This chapter has taken a careful look at ways in which you can optimize your success in such problem-based courses. Continuing the theme of you as a Good Strategy User, the chapter began by listing self-management strategies that stress the importance of timely and constant reinforcement of ideas. The questions that you choose to solve, your time management, and your use of resources are as important as the thinking strategies that lead to your eventually solving the problems.

Three specific thinking strategies were described through examples: the concept summary strategy, the decision steps strategy, and the range of problems strategy. Applied regularly, these three strategies can lead to sound understanding and retention of science concepts and processes.

In addition to theoretical problem solving, many problem-solving courses include a laboratory component. This chapter has stressed how important it is for you to be well prepared and to use your time wisely in the lab. If you can leave each lab with most, if not all, of the necessary work completed, you will have made strategic use of your time and resources.

 **WEB ALERT!**

Dawson College
Montreal, Quebec
http://dept.dawsoncollege.qc.ca/lc/problem.html
Learning by Problem Solving. Also go back one screen for Learning from Lab Notes.

Saint Louis University
St. Louis, Missouri
http://euler.slu.edu/Dept/SuccessinMath.html
Success in Mathematics includes "Math Study Skills" and "Problem Solving."

Nipissing University
North Bay, Ontario
www.nipissingu.ca/documents.cfm?itemid=6778
Math Study Skills.

CHAPTER ENDNOTES

1. Zajchowski, R., & Martin, J. (1993). Differences in the problem solving of stronger and weaker novices in physics: Knowledge, strategies or knowledge structure? *Journal of Research in Science Teaching, 5,* 459–470.
2. Zajchowski, R. & Martin, J. (1994). Improving the problem-solving performance of weaker physics novices. Poster presented at the annual meeting of the American Educational Research Association, New Orleans, 1994.
3. Based on steps by Dr. Colin Baird.
4. The decision steps that are associated with the concept of related rates have been written out separately and then applied to this problem. Assistance for this example was provided by Dr. Patricia Wrean of Camosun College.

Chapter 8

FOCUS ON THE SOCIAL SCIENCES AND HUMANITIES

LEARNING OBJECTIVES

The purpose of this chapter is for you to:

- Recognize and strategically organize academic arguments.
- Apply specific strategies for literature courses.
- Apply strategies for learning a second language.

The social sciences and humanities encompass disciplines that study the human condition. The social sciences include subject areas such as sociology, psychology, and political science, all of which seek to explain complex individual and societal behaviour and relationships. Although each subject area in the social sciences has its own distinct focus, methods of enquiry for all subject areas follow the scientific method. This means that investigations must rigorously define, examine, measure, and evaluate all aspects of the study before any conclusions can be considered to be valid. Subject areas in the humanities, such as literature, languages, and philosophy, explore all facets of culture as well as expressions of human creativity.

Because many of the disciplines in the social sciences and humanities have evolved from shared beginnings, you may well find yourself studying similar material in several of your courses, especially at the introductory level and in theory courses. It is the variety of focus, perspective, and approach to a universal subject matter that makes these fascinating areas of study.

This chapter looks at three key elements in the study of the social sciences and humanities:

- Evaluating academic arguments
- Strategies for literature courses
- Strategies for second-language learning

EVALUATING ACADEMIC ARGUMENTS

Academics love to argue; in fact, the key goal of their academic work is to question aspects of the world around them. As academics in the social sciences and humanities search for expressions and explanations of human behaviour, their studies are confounded by a whole variety of factors: the individuality of people; difficulty in studying internal human processes; freedom of choice; complexity of groups; and cultural diversity. This is why there is ongoing debate about so many issues.

At an everyday level you are, no doubt, already familiar with argumentative reasoning. You will have heard people debating a wide variety of issues ranging from which hockey team will win the Stanley Cup to the best way to eliminate Canada's national debt. The main difference between this everyday form of argument and the academic variety is that the latter must be vigorously and rigorously evaluated. You, as a Good Strategy User, need to develop strategies to recognize academic arguments in your texts or lectures so that you can evaluate and assess their significance.

Test questions often require that you recall important elements of academic arguments or apply the ideas of a specific argument to a new situation. To be well prepared for your tests, you can structure and memorize these elements by employing the pattern of an academic argument. Recall from Chapter 6, "Effective Memory," that efficient memory structures require that you organize key information on three different levels, and these levels can be applied to academic arguments: a title or label for the argument; general categories of information in the argument; and specific details that describe and explain the argument.

Titles that introduce academic arguments are usually easy to find, as they are among the headings in your course outline and/or textbook, and it is not uncommon for the title of the argument to be phrased as a question. When you read a heading in your text, or when your instructor poses a question in class, track carefully to see if an academic argument is being introduced.

There are five general categories of information in the checklist for academic arguments in the social sciences and humanities. These categories are your guide to selecting specific information or details for an argument:

1. The essence of the argument
2. Definitions of key terms
3. Evidence to support the argument, sometimes with examples
4. Conclusions
5. Counter arguments and/or connections to other topics

Read through the following example[1] (Table 8.1) for an academic argument that you might be asked to learn in your introductory psychology class. The specifics of the argument are guided by the pattern of five general categories noted above.

YOUR EXAMPLE OF AN ACADEMIC ARGUMENT

For one of your social sciences or humanities courses, create a memory structure for an academic argument that you have studied in a lecture or text reading. Use Table 8.2 on page 134 to help you fill in the details.

STRATEGIES FOR LITERATURE COURSES

As a student in a literature class, the one thing that you can be very sure of is that you will be expected to do a lot of reading, most likely over a very wide range of materials, and possibly including a combination of novels, plays, and poems. You will also be expected to produce quite a lot of writing in the course. As a Good Strategy User, you need to think through your expectations of any literature course and plan how you will approach it, so you can optimize your enjoyment, learning, and success in the course. By taking a strategic approach to your literature courses, you can meet all of your goals.

TABLE 8.1   Memory Structure for an Academic Argument

TITLE OF THE ARGUMENT: WHAT MAKES A FACE ATTRACTIVE?	
COMPONENTS	SPECIFIC INFORMATION
THE ESSENCE OF THE ARGUMENT	Langlois & Roggman (1990) and Langlois et al. (1994) argue that people are programmed to prefer faces that are *average* representations of faces in the population
DEFINITIONS OF KEY TERMS	An **average face**: is not a common, typical, or frequently occurring face but is a prototypical face **Prototypical face**: a face that is a good representation of the category "faces"
EVIDENCE TO SUPPORT THE ARGUMENT AND EXAMPLES	– People were asked to rate the attractiveness of average faces that were generated electronically on a computer. – To create these faces, hundreds of individual black and white photographs, composed of either male or female Caucasians, Asians, and Hispanics, were scanned into a computer and digitized into matrices of individual grey values. – Participants in the study were shown faces of individuals as well as of composites that averaged the grey values across a large number of individuals—a type of "prototype" face. – People generally rated the composite faces as more attractive than the individual faces.
CONCLUSIONS	Langlois and Roggman offer two speculative conclusions for the average face being preferred: 1. It is linked to survival in newborn infants as being easier for them to recognize as a face. 2. An individual with "average" features is less likely to harbour potentially harmful genetic mutations.
COUNTER ARGUMENTS/ CONNECTIONS TO OTHER TOPICS	Two other perspectives have been used to explain the concept of attractiveness: 1. An evolutionary perspective links attractiveness to success in mating and offspring rearing, which transcends cultural boundaries. 2. There is a strong social bias—fashions of attractiveness come and go, but, again, there is an element of cultural universality in appreciating an attractive face at any point in time.

TABLE 8.2   Your Own Example for an Academic Argument

TITLE OF THE ARGUMENT:	
COMPONENTS	SPECIFIC INFORMATION
THE ESSENCE OF THE ARGUMENT	
DEFINITIONS OF KEY TERMS	
EVIDENCE TO SUPPORT THE ARGUMENT AND EXAMPLES	
CONCLUSIONS	
COUNTER ARGUMENTS/ CONNECTIONS TO OTHER TOPICS	

PLAN AN EARLY START

It is not uncommon for literature courses, especially survey courses, to cover at least one item per week. If at all possible, try to read at least a few of the assigned materials before your course begins. Instructors of literature courses usually make the reading lists available when course selection is taking place. If a reading list is not available at that time, check out the course website or ask at the instructor's or department office. You don't have to attempt to read everything before the course begins, but any item you complete can give you a head start in keeping up with the load.

SEEK OUT GUIDELINES FROM YOUR INSTRUCTOR

Although you should read all of the assigned works in your course, it may be appropriate to choose several works to process very thoroughly and others more lightly. Seek out any guidelines that your instructor has written into your course outline or discussed in class. That is, know early in the course whether or not your essay assignments and exams will cover every work or, more likely, will offer you a choice of questions. If there is choice, then you can target certain works for more attention rather than trying to know everything at the same level. However, make sure that you do have enough variety in your repertoire, as you will not impress your instructor if you are using a limited set of examples in your work. Ideally, you should reference different works to illustrate each question you answer on an exam.

MEET YOUR AUTHORS

Find out something of the history and background of the authors represented in your course. Your library will have literary encyclopedias with biographies on key authors. The Internet is another source for biographies, but if you do use the Internet try to assess the quality of the website that you are visiting. Excellent information is available online from publishers, national libraries, and major educational institutions. It does not take long to find out general background on your authors, and it can help put their writing into a meaningful context.

AIM TO READ FOR ENJOYMENT AS WELL AS FOR STUDY

When reading any novel, play, or poem, put yourself in the role of general reader first and student second. You need to feel your emotional response to this literary work as well as your rational understanding of it. If you allow yourself to get carried into the story or moved by characters or events, you are more likely to have something very personal to contribute to your academic discussion of the work in your essay or exam.

KNOW THE KEY LITERARY ELEMENTS

Authors enrich their writing through a variety of devices, and it is these literary elements that your instructor will introduce in class and that you will discuss and interpret in your papers and exams. Each instructor will emphasize certain elements, so listen carefully for those that are stressed in your course, and make sure to record them in your notes.

Make yourself a reminder of the literary elements, perhaps on a flash card, adding to your list as each is introduced in turn. Keep your list handy and, to tune your awareness, look it over at the beginning of each lecture and before reading. You may need to develop a separate list for the three major categories of literary works in your course: novels, plays, and poetry. Although many of the elements are common to all three, there are some specific differences. The following list was developed for use with novels:

- **Genre:** category or type of literary work
- **Narrative:** the story, plot, or connection of events running through the work; causality
- **Setting:** place; time; an event; combination of people and things
- **Theme:** main idea or meaning of the novel; thesis
- **Characters:** created entities or personalities with a role in the novel—human, animal, object, real or imaginary
- **Voice:** teller of the story—first person/narrator, multiple voices, third person
- **Tone:** mood; atmosphere; feeling; connectivity
- **Imagery/symbolism:** use of images and symbols—things that encapsulate, capture, or typically represent a concept; allegory; metaphor; simile
- **Culture/philosophy:** learned traditions; ethnicity; way of life; fundamental beliefs
- **Emotions:** conflict; love; hatred; despair; tragedy; hope; confusion
- **Style:** exposition; method of delivery—dialogue, vocabulary, sentences and fragments; alliteration; assonance

KNOW AND UNDERSTAND CRITICAL PERSPECTIVES

Scholars have proposed many different theories to explain literature, and you will need to come to grips with recognizing and understanding them, as well as applying them to a variety of literary works. As with the literary devices listed above, you will need to track theories as they are introduced in your lectures or texts. In addition, you might create a learning aid that lists and summarizes all of the theories. This will help you to connect terms and their definitions to their relevant theories. This learning aid might be a file on your computer that you append as each new theory is introduced. You can then keep a current paper copy of this file with your class notes so you have the information for easy reference. File cards are another option, with each card assigned to an individual theory. Whatever your system, there are a number of elements of theories that you need to include in your summary:

- Name or title of the theory
- Main proponents of the theory
- Origins of the theory: date or time period, and rationale behind the theory
- Key terms/concepts with definitions
- Links/overlap with other theories
- Applications to selected works

ACTIVELY READ FOR THESIS STATEMENTS

As you read a literary work and gradually absorb its form and message, always be thinking about your interpretations and possible thesis statements. (See Chapter 10, "Writing Research Papers," for more on thesis statements.) You will have to write papers or answer exam questions in your literature course, and these will always require a clearly stated thesis. Thesis statements often evolve out of an examination of questions and relationships. As you read a work, first identify the literary elements most relevant to the work and your reading and analysis of it. For each element, generate questions and read to answer them. For example, if your focus is on "tone," you might ask yourself:

What feelings or meanings are being conveyed—amusement, anger, uncertainty, fear, irony—and how do they contribute to the narrative?

How do the various settings for this story relate to changes in tone?

How is tone used as an element in character development?

Do changes of tone predict significant events in the plot?

In addition to asking questions based on the literary elements, think about any relationships revealed in the work: process or evolution; cause and effect; correlations; comparisons and contrasts; defining moments. By reading actively to generate theses, you will gradually develop confidence in your judgment and ability to come up with the definitive thesis statement.

DEVELOP AN EFFECTIVE RECORDING SYSTEM

One of the downsides of getting absorbed in a work of literature is that you might forget to mark items that you want to find again, especially in books or plays. Most of us have had that frustrating experience of frantically flipping pages while looking for that one phrase that would fit perfectly into our paper. How can you avoid this problem without having to interrupt your reading constantly to make notes?

There are a number of possible solutions to identifying key sections efficiently, most of which work best if you actually own the book rather than having borrowed it from a library or friend. You can turn down the corner of a page; this is the fastest method. You can keep a pencil in hand and use it to mark a passage quickly. Perhaps the best method is to add small sticky notes to the edge of the page; they have the added advantage of allowing you to annotate later, colour code different types of information, and place them adjacent to notable items.

When you have finished a sizeable section of the work, make a more complete set of summary notes, either in a computer file or in a notebook. In addition to a brief summary of characters, setting, and plot, identify some of the other major elements in the work. For each, either make up some questions to organize your thinking, or jot down a summary of some key ideas that you have.

Some works may be adequately summarized using graphic organizers to display main relationships in the story (see Figures 8.1[2] and 8.2[3]). Graphic organizers are more visual and, consequently, more memorable than straight text. However, they work best if you are very familiar with a work and use the organizer to stimulate recall of additional details. There are many options for layout. Check back to the examples in Chapter 4, "Learning from Lectures." It is up to you to find a style that you think best suits the work.

If you get additional credit for being able to quote directly from literary works, make a few flash cards of short direct quotes that you think you may be able to use, and periodically look over them to put them into your long-term memory. However, be very selective with this strategy, as it can be time consuming and may not have a lot of payoff if you cannot match the quote with a relevant concept.

DEVELOP YOUR OWN OPINIONS BEFORE CONSULTING SECONDARY SOURCES

Reading a novel is a very personal experience; you may love a particular novel while your neighbour in class absolutely detests it. The main challenge of a literature course is for you to be able to present evidence to support your own point of view, whatever it may be. Read a novel to develop your own interpretation and opinions about it before going

FIGURE 8.1   Summary for *Unless* by Carol Shields

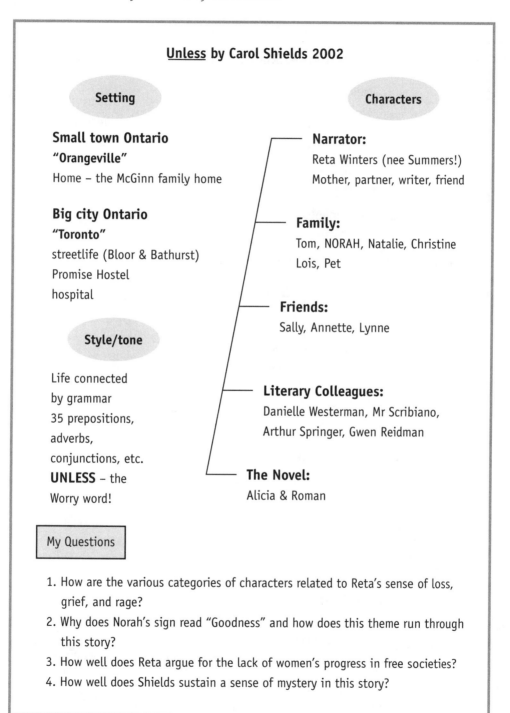

Unless by Carol Shields 2002

Setting

Small town Ontario
"Orangeville"
Home – the McGinn family home

Big city Ontario
"Toronto"
streetlife (Bloor & Bathurst)
Promise Hostel
hospital

Style/tone

Life connected
by grammar
35 prepositions,
adverbs,
conjunctions, etc.
UNLESS – the
Worry word!

Characters

Narrator:
Reta Winters (nee Summers!)
Mother, partner, writer, friend

Family:
Tom, NORAH, Natalie, Christine
Lois, Pet

Friends:
Sally, Annette, Lynne

Literary Colleagues:
Danielle Westerman, Mr Scribiano,
Arthur Springer, Gwen Reidman

The Novel:
Alicia & Roman

My Questions

1. How are the various categories of characters related to Reta's sense of loss, grief, and rage?
2. Why does Norah's sign read "Goodness" and how does this theme run through this story?
3. How well does Reta argue for the lack of women's progress in free societies?
4. How well does Shields sustain a sense of mystery in this story?

FIGURE 8.2   Summary for *The In-between World of Vikram Lall* by M. G. Vassanj

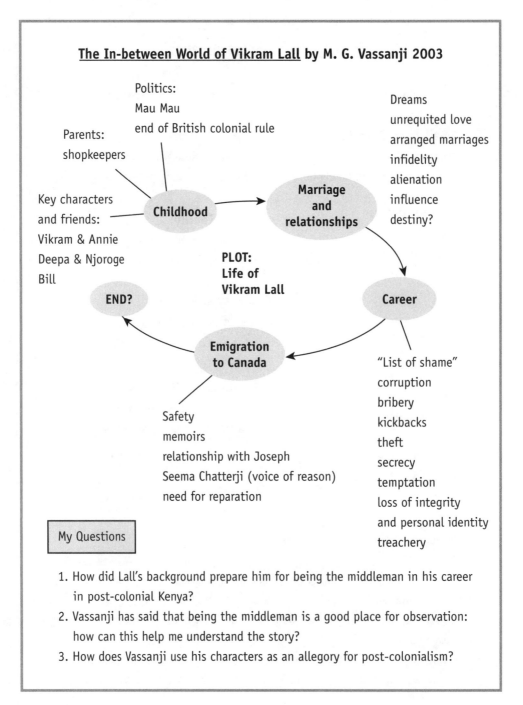

to any secondary sources to find out more about the work. There are many reviews of books on the Internet—whole websites are dedicated to them; publishers offer reading guides and commentary about books in their catalogues; many booksellers also post reviews, either from their staff or customers. It is not difficult to find a plethora of materials out there, but use them appropriately to your own learning goals. You are in this literature course to develop your own critical-thinking skills, and by reading and responding to a work before consulting other sources you will optimize your own learning.

LEARNING A SECOND LANGUAGE

Most of us these days hear languages other than our own first language on a daily basis, through multicultural programming on TV or by overhearing people talking to each other in the community. Many of you reading this book will already speak more than one language and may do so fluently on a daily basis. Language courses at all levels are in greater demand than ever before as students recognize their advantages in the modern workplace, for travel, in fostering appreciation of other cultures, and as a way of increasing personal satisfaction and self-confidence.

You may have chosen to learn a second or third language for any of the above reasons, or it may be that you need the credit as a mandatory requirement in your social sciences or humanities program. If you self-selected to take a language course, you will likely be looking forward to it and eager to get started. If you had no choice but to register for the course for progression requirements, you may be feeling some anxiety, wondering how you will meet the challenge. Whatever your background, a strategic approach can help you on the road to success with learning your second language. Read through and reflect on the suggested strategies, and choose which to apply to your own language learning.

AIM FOR A POSITIVE PERSONAL ATTITUDE

- ☑ Get acquainted with the culture associated with the language by talking to another student from a country where that language is spoken.
- ☑ Know why you are taking the course, and write down some personal goals specifying what you hope to gain from it.
- ☑ Go to the first class intending to be an active participant.
- ☑ If you have a friend in class, give each other mutual support.
- ☑ Allow yourself to take chances and not worry if you make mistakes as you use your new language.

DEVELOP YOUR READINESS FOR LEARNING

☑ Listen to your new language by tuning in to a TV show for a while and just listening to the pace and rhythm of the language.

☑ Pick up a magazine or book or find a website in your target language and see how the language looks written down.

☑ Check through an English grammar and remind yourself of the parts of language in English.

☑ Look over your course outline and the website for the course.

☑ Introduce yourself to your instructor and ask questions based on your early reading of the course outline.

MANAGE YOUR TIME WELL

☑ Always attend class and work on assignments promptly.

☑ Spend time each day studying for your language course.

☑ Use several small blocks of time each day, rather than one large chunk.

☑ Study when you are feeling mentally alert—not tired.

☑ Every week, spend some study time on review of previous weeks' units.

GRADUALLY EXPAND YOUR VOCABULARY

☑ As much as possible, learn your vocabulary in context rather than as isolated words.

☑ Develop a system for noting new vocabulary, such as making lists—perhaps on flash cards—using categories to organize them.

☑ If you find some words difficult to remember, use some memory devices, such as colour or associations to make them stick—and self-test on a regular basis.

☑ Target a few new words to build into your repertoire and consciously choose to use them while speaking or writing. These do not have to be assignments; you can write a short story or speak a few sentences to practise.

☑ Use your e-mail or a chat room to communicate by computer with others in your class. Your focus should be on communicating ideas rather than on being totally accurate.

PRACTISE SPEAKING THE LANGUAGE AT EVERY OPPORTUNITY

☑ Learn some basic expressions for greeting people and asking how they are, and use them with others in your class as part of your daily interaction.

☑ Regularly, use fairly simple sentence constructions that you feel you can handle. There is plenty of time to get more sophisticated later on.

☑ Study out loud even when you are reading or writing for the course. This will involve mouth movements and sound, and the more senses you use in learning the more memory you will develop.

☑ Regularly practise basic sounds. Each language has its own unique sounds in pronunciation, and as an adult it takes a lot of practise to be able to reproduce these.

☑ Take every opportunity to speak the language, focusing on what you want to communicate and not worrying about mistakes.

Develop Excellent Listening Skills

☑ Always sit near the front of the class, where you can listen without too many external distractions.

☑ Don't expect to understand everything you hear. If you are asked a question and do not understand, don't panic; ask for the question to be repeated—this will be one of the stock phrases that you have learned of course!

☑ Keep relaxed in class; effective listening can take a lot of mental and physical energy.

☑ When another student is asked a question, plan an answer that you would have given to that question, and think it through silently but completely.

☑ Listen to a variety of resources: TV; films; other students.

Enhance Your Memory

☑ Use flash cards and self-test.

☑ Use repetition, especially with anything you are having difficulty with.

☑ Work with a variety of materials and in a variety of modes.

☑ Make every effort to use the language, whether you are listening, speaking, or reading.

☑ Give it time. Gradually over time, with regular effort and practice, some of the more basic elements will become automatic and will not require effort. Then you can build on this base and make substantial progress.

Consolidate Your Knowledge of Grammar

☑ Regularly complete any exercises that you are assigned, and for each one take note of new grammatical elements or constructions.

☑ Having refreshed your English grammar, you can now seek out major differences and similarities in construction between your two languages.

☑ Don't get too complicated with your speaking and writing. Just make sure that you are familiar with some fairly simple sentence constructions, and regularly practise using them.

☑ Memorize and use irregular verbs and idiomatic phrases that cannot be directly translated.

☑ Review past grammar lessons regularly.

MAKE THE MOST OF READING

☑ Use your computer to practise your reading skills; find an interesting website and see how much of it you can decipher.

☑ With a reading assignment, first check over the vocabulary list. Read over the passage one or two times, fairly quickly, trying to get a sense of the meaning. Don't take it one word at a time.

☑ Try to guess at the meaning of new vocabulary in context rather than immediately going to a dictionary.

☑ Examine a few sentences for consistency; see how the nouns and verbs agree and how the adjectives and adverbs expand the meaning. Pay close attention to such aspects as gender, accents, and colloquial phrases.

☑ Read a novel in your new language, and discuss it with a friend. Pay attention to what it tells you about people and culture.

DIVERSITY OF CHOICE AND STRATEGIES

The social sciences and humanities offer you tremendous choice in the programs and courses available to you. The common link in this diversity is the human condition, which takes centre stage. For a broad educational experience, and if appropriate to your program, sample and choose from this diversity so that your academic skills can develop in directions that will be of great benefit in the years to come.

This chapter first examined the elements in academic arguments, emphasizing a systematic approach to discussion and debate. It went on to present a wide array of learning strategies for literature courses and for learning a second language, emphasizing once again the diverse nature of the social sciences and humanities and the opportunities they offer you to develop essential skills. Chapters 10 and 11 continue this theme as they explore in more detail two more areas of key importance: writing research papers and giving class presentations and seminars.

WEB ALERT!

University of New Brunswick
Fredericton, New Brunswick
http://extend.unb.ca/wss/crittext.htm#int
QuickNotes on Critical Thinking.

Purdue University
West Lafayette, Indiana
www.sla.purdue.edu/academic/engl/theory
Introductory Guide to Critical Theory.

The University of Minnesota: Twin Cities
Minneapolis/St. Paul, Minnesota
www.ucs.umn.edu/lasc/handouts/strategieslearning.html
Foreign Languages. Click on both "Strategies for Learning a Second Language" and "Study Tips on Foreign Languages: A Summary of Do's and Don'ts."

CHAPTER ENDNOTES

1. Example from *Psychology: The Adaptive Mind,* 2nd Cdn ed. (p. 541), by J. S. Nairne, D. S. Lindsay, D. L. Paulus, & M. S. Smith, 2004, Scarborough ON: Thomson Nelson.
2. Based on *Unless,* by C. Shields, 2002. Toronto: Random House.
3. Based on *The In-between World of Vikram Lall,* by M. G. Vassanji, 2003, Toronto: Doubleday Canada.

Chapter 9

MANAGING THE STRESS OF BEING A STUDENT

LEARNING OBJECTIVES

The purpose of this chapter is for you to:

- Understand the stress factors in academic settings.
- Learn how to identify your symptoms of stress.
- Identify strategies that can help you to cope with stress.
- Recognize how to achieve good concentration.

As you start each new academic year, you can anticipate some of the challenges ahead, but you cannot predict all of the demands of your courses nor can you predict your relationships with individual instructors and students. This uncertainty can be exciting as long as you can make plans that prepare you to be flexible. However, if you perceive the demands of a particular situation to be overwhelming, you may start to experience symptoms of stress as you try to balance the demands of being a student with your capacity to sustain physical and mental wear and tear.

This chapter discusses how you can recognize your own responses to stress, both emotional and physical. It prompts you to realize that your stress responses frequently reflect your mental messages about the demands of specific events and situations. This chapter also presents a variety of strategies that you can practise in order to reduce the psychological and physical symptoms of stress and maintain your health and energy throughout the year. If you can maintain a schedule that gives you enough time to rest, to eat balanced meals, and to find effective ways of relieving tension, you will feel more motivated to study and more in control of your school experience.

WHAT IS STRESS?

Stress usually starts with feelings of emotional discomfort and concern about not being able to cope. You may experience physical symptoms of stress, such as loss of appetite, sleeplessness, headaches, and sweating. You may also find that you catch cold and flu more often. At a psychological level, you may start to feel helpless, anxious, or afraid of losing personal control and motivation to be a successful student. While you may recognize that such feelings can change your mood because of a number of subtle chemical changes in the brain, you may not realize that these chemical changes, in turn, affect the strength of your immune system and can lower your body's ability to cope with day-to-day strain and to fight off infection.[1]

Individuals can interpret the same situation very differently. For example, a snowstorm is not stressful to a skier, but it is to someone who has to drive any distance to an important meeting. The skier will probably experience what Hans Selye[2] has described as "eu-stress"—a positive response as she looks forward to a day on the ski slopes. The driver, however, may experience distress—a negative response to the snowstorm as he anticipates being unable to reach the meeting on time. Therefore, you may find that your reaction to academic stress is different from that of your friends, even though they may be in almost the same situation. For example, some of your friends may look forward to the chance to perform on a test while others sense that the test is a threat that might exceed their intellectual and personal resources. The former students will get some positive energy and focus, while the latter may be very distracted and unable to concentrate.

The positive message here is that you *can* learn to think about challenging and unexpected situations in a more constructive way so that you can control your response to them. When you are devising strategies to deal with stress, it is important to recognize the importance of your perceptions about events going on around you.

PSYCHOLOGICAL STRATEGIES FOR COPING WITH STRESS

As already explained, the way you think about events can have a powerful influence on whether you find them stressful. Since your thoughts influence your response to stress, try to recognize your inner dialogue about day-to-day demands and expectations. Many of us are not aware of our "self-talk" and do not realize how self-defeating it may be. For example, if you dread certain occasions and fear their possible consequences (e.g., presenting a seminar), it may be difficult to control your negative reactions and to work on preparing an effective seminar presentation. Compare your mental messages about studying with thoughts about something that you really enjoy. Record what your thoughts might be in the situations listed in Table 9.1.

TABLE 9.1   Your Recorded Thoughts

YOUR EXPERIENCE	STUDY ACTIVITY (E.G., THOUGHTS WHILE WRITING AN IN-CLASS TEST)	LEISURE ACTIVITY (E.G., THOUGHTS WHILE PLAYING TENNIS WITH A FRIEND)
You make a mistake	"This could mean I will get a low grade in this course"	
You recognize your limitations to do well		
You consider the future consequences of this event		

When you are enjoying an activity, you are usually less concerned about making mistakes, your own limitations, or future consequences. In contrast, when you are anxious about your academic progress, your worries can distract your attention and interfere with learning. This may prompt you to take time out to rest, but that may be a temporary solution. You still have to find a way to put positive energy into studying. One self-management strategy that can help is to focus your thoughts on the present with statements such as *"What's involved here?"* or *"What's the next step?"*

PHYSICAL STRATEGIES FOR COPING WITH STRESS

In addition to considering the psychological aspects of stress, it is also important to evaluate how to keep in good physical shape to handle pressure. Do you make time to exercise to give you time to relax both mentally and physically? Regular exercise improves your attitude as well as your health and stamina.

Find Ways to Become a More Relaxed Person

☑ Learn relaxation techniques to reduce tension. You can practise deep breathing or yoga, take a warm bath, or listen to some of your favourite music.

☑ Learn to use techniques for good concentration (see p. 150), and take regular and planned breaks from studying.

☑ If you begin to panic, remove yourself from the source of stress. Get up from your desk and take a short walk.

☑ Take up a sport, hobby, or part-time interest that will help you to relax.

Develop a Healthy Lifestyle Ensuring That You Eat and Sleep Regularly

☑ Plan to eat with friends to maintain your social contacts.

☑ Take a positive attitude toward your body image. Being preoccupied with your weight or appearance can be a source of a lot of stress.

☑ Try to eat a variety of foods necessary for a regularly balanced diet.

☑ Maintain a sensible sleep routine. Don't try to escape stress by oversleeping during the day.

TAKING CONTROL OF STRESS

If you are able to understand your response to stress and have some strategies at your disposal for dealing with stress when necessary, you will start to feel more optimistic. At this point you can expect to:

- Experience a sense of control over your life.
- Be able to identify a network of individuals who can provide you with necessary support.
- Take a flexible approach to unexpected events.
- Regularly engage in a hobby, sport, or outside interest.

However, many students do find that stress is a debilitating factor at some time or another in their lives, and there may be times when you feel that your problems are overwhelming. However hard you try, you can't shake off severe anxiety and depression. Remember that schools, colleges, and universities have professional staff who can help you. Sharing your worries and discussing solutions with another person, either a counsellor or a health professional, can make a positive difference. **Don't hesitate to seek help from others if you need it.**

CONCENTRATION

Poor concentration can be one very real source of stress. For example, you may find yourself dreaming about nonacademic issues while trying to study, even when you feel motivated to study. Concentration does not "just happen," and this section will address how to achieve better concentration and improved academic performance. Two or three hours of concentrated effort are worth a day of interrupted or haphazard study. Good Strategy Users focus on three components of concentration:

- Commitment
- Internal Distractions
- External Distractions

COMMITMENT

A crucial element to accomplishing your study goals is finding an appropriate out-of-class learning environment where you can avoid distraction, concentrate, and get things done.

- Find a quiet, comfortable place to study.
- Make sure that you have all the necessary materials and equipment.
- Check your study tasks for the day.
- Set a study goal for what you wish to accomplish in the next short time period (20 to 50 minutes).

Work at maintaining a real interest in your courses. Your level of commitment while studying is closely linked to your interest in the subject matter, the way in which the course is taught, and whether the course is optional or mandatory. The following strategies can help you to maintain a high level of commitment to a course:

- Find out as much as you can about a course before choosing to take it. Read the calendar description, talk to the instructor, and, if possible, talk to students who have taken the course. Check that your background is adequate to handle the course without any major problems and that you feel confident about being able to manage the workload.
- Assess the contribution that the course will make to your general knowledge, to your degree program, and to possible career choices. Your commitment will be stronger if you have a clear idea about the benefits of the course.
- Know the rules and regulations governing the course. If you have a clear idea of whether or not you can withdraw from a course if things go poorly, you will not feel so trapped and be better able to give it a reasonable effort.
- Try to generate interest in a required course. You might try to find out about the history of the course or talk about it with someone who seems to enjoy it.
- If you anticipate any problems, you may wish to be part of a study group. In difficult courses, it can be helpful to meet to share ideas and study tasks.
- Try to work regularly at the course. It is difficult to maintain a high level of commitment when you fall behind and get overwhelmed by the amount of work.

INTERNAL DISTRACTIONS

Your determination to pursue your studying in an active way can be gauged by whether you can use some of the following self-management strategies to control internal distractions:

- Define a specific objective to be completed in a limited time frame. Avoid taking a vague approach that just states a good intention, such as "I'll do as much as I can on Tuesday evening." In contrast, set content- and strategy-oriented goals together with a time goal (see p. 20 in Chapter 2, "Resources for Strategic Learners"), and say, "I'm going to read five pages of sociology by first surveying and then reading each section to extract the main ideas, and I am aiming to accomplish this in 30 minutes." This can give you realistic and measurable goals to work toward.

- Set up a method of self-testing the work you have covered in any hour. Knowing that you have to self-test will keep your focus on the task. The self-testing activities will increase your ability to recall material.
- When your mind wanders from the topic at hand, put a checkmark on a piece of paper. Monitor the number of checkmarks you accumulate over several study sessions to assess whether your attention span is improving.
- Apply "thought stopping" when you find yourself daydreaming. Say "STOP" mentally and then redirect your attention back to your work.
- Use problem-solving techniques to deal with a persistently disturbing thought, such as "Should I be looking for a part-time job?"
  - ☑ Move away from your study task.
  - ☑ Decide what is bothering you.
  - ☑ Look at why the issue is nagging at you.
  - ☑ List the pros and cons of possible solutions to the problem.
  - ☑ Decide whether you can handle the issue by yourself or if you need to consult with others.
  - ☑ Plan when and how to deal with this particular problem. Make a note of it, and then return to your studying.

EXTERNAL DISTRACTIONS

Setting the environment for study is important to managing concentration. You will lose concentration while studying if you are physically uncomfortable. You may be too hot, too hungry, or too full. The light level may be straining your eyes, or the position in which you are studying may cause your neck or back to hurt. You may find yourself constantly interrupted by noise or by other people wanting your attention. Consequently, you may find that you begin to think about a whole range of different things, none of them associated with your course material. Find a time and place for studying with few distractions where it is easier for you to control your attention. Most of us can focus on only one main train of thought at a time. In your study experience, how difficult do you find it to ignore the distractions listed in Table 9.2?

If you find that you can be distracted fairly easily, try the following ideas to modify your learning environment:

- Clear your desk of souvenirs, pictures, and so on. These can be extremely distracting.
- Arrange your desk so that it faces a blank wall. Even your studying should be more interesting than a blank wall!

TABLE 9.2   Monitor Your Distractions

		EASY TO IGNORE	MORE DIFFICULT TO IGNORE	IMPOSSIBLE TO IGNORE
1.	Hearing a conversation near your desk.			
2.	Sensing doors opening and shutting.			
3.	Hearing the radio or TV in the room.			
4.	Noticing traffic outside the room.			
5.	Hearing specific loud noises (e.g., a siren).			
6.	Being interrupted by someone.			

- Know which libraries suit you. Experiment until you find the ones in which you prefer to study at certain times of day.
- Have the right level of noise in the background. Try different situations such as a moderate level of "white noise" or complete silence.

YOUR CONCENTRATION PROFILE

Assume that you want to give your full concentration to a task. In the space below, describe the ideal situation that will allow you complete concentration.

_____

_____

_____

At one time or another, we all have problems concentrating on a task. Imagine you are reading a chapter in a chemistry or sociology text. Even though the environment is conducive to studying, after 20 minutes you feel like giving up because you realize that you are not getting anything out of it. List some possible reasons for this.

_____

_____

_____

WHAT ARE YOUR SUGGESTIONS FOR MANAGING STRESS?

If you were asked to help students with managing their stress, what strategies would you suggest? In this exercise, suggested strategies for Connie have been provided as a model. Complete the exercise by writing down three strategies for each of the problems that Raj, Chris, and Tony have presented to you.

Connie had started back to school with such high hopes. It had been 20 years since she had been in school. This first essay was such a struggle, and her grade reflects that. She barely passed and is feeling very stressed out. How can she get her confidence back?

1. Connie checks her self-talk. She had told herself that she must get an A grade on this paper. She recognizes that it was asking a lot for a first paper.

2. She decides that the next step is to go and talk to the instructor so that she can find out more about the problems in her paper. She arranges for an appointment.

3. Connie checks out the writing skills clinic resources so that she knows what help is available when she has to write her next paper.

Raj is daydreaming in the library again. Every time he hears someone go by, he looks up. Then he tries to focus again on reading about the Canadian Constitution. He can hardly wait for 5:00 p.m. so he can pack up and go home. How can Raj take more control over his concentration?

1. _____

   _____

2. _____

   _____

3. _____

   _____

Chris is having problems sleeping because she has so much to do with all of her course work, a part-time job, and dealing with some problems back home. Now she just isn't feeling well and her energy level seems so low. What lifestyle choices can Chris make to try to maintain good health?

1. _____

_____

2. _____

_____

3. _____

_____

Tony is not at all sure that college is where he wants to be. He thought that he had chosen his program well but now he is starting to have doubts. He would at least like to get through this year successfully to keep his options open. Can you suggest ways in which Tony can increase his commitment to his program to give himself a better chance of success?

1. _____

_____

2. _____

_____

3. _____

_____

MANAGING YOUR LEVEL OF STRESS

This chapter has discussed how you can become more aware of your responses to pressure and stress. It presented self-management strategies, both psychological and physical, to help you cope with symptoms of stress. If you can commit yourself to your studies and avoid internal and external distractions, you will be more likely to achieve good concentration and effective thinking strategies. This chapter also recommended that if you continue to feel anxious about the demands of your academic courses you should ask for help in assessing how to develop strategies to achieve better concentration and control over your response to the demands of being a successful student.

The chapters that you have read so far in this book have introduced you to the idea of good strategy use and have presented many strategies for self-management and for thinking about academic tasks in a wide variety of settings. The last part of this book turns now to those tasks where you will apply much of what you have learned in your courses. Part 4 is all about putting in a successful performance.

w w w WEB ALERT!

Acadia University
Wolfville, Nova Scotia
http://admin.acadiau.ca/counsel/studyskills/topics/copestress.html
What Is Stress?

Fleming College
Peterborough, Ontario
http://fleming0.flemingc.on.ca/lrc/referral/counsel/study.htm
Concentration.

University of Toronto
Toronto, Ontario
www.calss.utoronto.ca/pamphlets/coping.htm
Coping with Stress at University: Exams.

CHAPTER ENDNOTES

1. Rice, P. L. (1999). *Stress and health*. Florence, KY: Thomson: Brooks/Cole, 12–13.
2. Selye, H. (1978). *The stress of life* (2nd ed.). New York: McGraw-Hill.

Part 4

Chapter 10

WRITING RESEARCH PAPERS

LEARNING OBJECTIVES

The purpose of this chapter is for you to:
- Recognize the key features of a good research paper.
- Learn how to analyze your writing assignment.
- Recognize the importance of structure in a well-written paper.
- Learn about the six stages required for completing a research paper.
- Assess your own performance.
- Learn about self-help books on effective writing.

Aresearch paper challenges you to explain your ideas on a topic in a clear and logical manner and to help your reader acquire new insights. It's not an easy task to develop and synthesize information in a cohesive way within a reasonable time frame. To write a good research paper, you need to explore and understand the topic, plan an outline, write a draft, and then revise and polish your final version.

This chapter starts by identifying features of a good research paper. It goes on to outline the steps that you, as a Good Strategy User, can take to express your personal ideas within the limits set up by your instructor. At each stage in the writing process, you have to recognize not only what is expected, but also what you can achieve in the time available.

FEATURES OF A GOOD RESEARCH PAPER

Being able to write well is one of the most important skills that you will acquire as a student. No one essay or research paper is ever the last word or the best way of writing about a topic. If you can keep an open mind to the feedback you receive and approach each assignment with a strategic plan, you can learn to write a convincing composition and gain confidence in your writing ability. First, let's look at some of the important features of a good research paper.

- Cohesive Analysis
- Consistent Thesis
- Documented and Relevant Sources
- Clear and Logical Organization
- Effective Language and Presentation
- Correct Formatting, Spelling, and Grammar

COHESIVE ANALYSIS

A good paper presents information in a cohesive, logical, and reasoned way so the reader can follow each idea from start to finish. It is generally not enough for you simply to describe or outline a topic; you need to pursue a sequence of ideas that reveals your analysis and point of view.

CONSISTENT THESIS

In its introduction, a research paper has a statement of opinion, often called the thesis. This is the argument you want to present in your paper, and it will control and focus the way you develop and sequence the main points. Therefore, every paragraph in your paper must relate directly to your chosen thesis. In the examples below, for instance, the final papers associated with each of these two thesis statements will be different although the general topic is the same—the ozone layer:

- If society takes responsibility for controlling the pollution in our environment, it may be possible to stop the depletion of the ozone layer.
- The depletion of the ozone layer is the number-one concern for society because, unless this problem can be solved, all other problems will be meaningless.

Documented and Relevant Sources

You need to ensure that you are using ideas and information from credible sources. You should begin by checking your institution's library holdings and the databases to which they subscribe. Most college and university libraries offer orientation sessions that will help you to learn about available sources, such as books and journals. The librarian will also introduce you to relevant catalogues and indexes and can advise you about alternative ways of referencing your sources. One advantage of the library is that, once you have located one suitable source by using the catalogue, you can browse the adjoining texts on the shelf for additional materials on the same topic.

Computers and the Internet have made it far easier for you to access information than ever before. Journal articles are more readily accessed through databases on the computer that allow you to locate many relevant titles, abstracts, and, sometimes, full papers. Again, consult with reference librarians if you do not have experience with finding references through key word searches as they can be quite sophisticated. However, be prepared for some frustration as your institution may not subscribe to the journal you are looking for and you may have to find alternative materials.

General Internet sources, in the main, do not meet the rigorous standards needed for an academic paper since many of them have not been reviewed before posting. If you do want to reference something from the Internet, check first with your instructor to find out whether he/she will accept the sources and how you should document them in your references.

If you are tackling a topic that is new to you, you may want to begin with a recent general survey of the topic, unless you know that an earlier book is the standard in the field. It's likely that the recent survey will provide references that will take you to other relevant reading. In many disciplines, it is enough to use only secondary sources such as survey texts or review articles in periodicals. However, in some subjects, the use of primary sources—for example, government documents or literary works—may also be required. Remember to credit all sources that contribute evidence to your argument.

CLEAR AND LOGICAL ORGANIZATION

A good research paper presents ideas that support the argument in a clear and organized sequence. You can refer to the next section, "Structure of a Research Paper," to remind you of the sequence that presents a clear argument.

Well-organized paragraphs will make a positive difference to the overall organization of the paper. The assertion, or topic sentence, generally appears at the beginning of each paragraph and tells the reader the exact topic of the paragraph. The rest of the paragraph explains what that assertion means, by defining the terms or clarifying the idea. It then provides evidence through details, examples, illustrations, and other types of proof.

Be selective about the sources of evidence you use so that they are consistent with your thesis and structure.

EFFECTIVE LANGUAGE AND PRESENTATION

A good paper is more impressive if it uses both vocabulary and sentence structure that present the ideas clearly. Make use of various resources (some are listed at the end of this chapter) that will help you eliminate jargon and pretentious language.

CORRECT FORMATTING, SPELLING, AND GRAMMAR

A good paper must use appropriate formatting and correct spelling and grammar. Check the instructions that you are given about formatting. Your instructor may have very clear expectations that you must follow. Use the spelling and grammar check on your computer to help you make your paper as accurate as possible, but do your own final read as well to double-check how your meaning is presented.

ANALYZING THE ASSIGNMENT

Every essay or research paper grows out of an assignment, and nearly every assignment (whether guided by an elaborate set of printed instructions, by a few brief suggestions from your instructor, or entirely by your own ideas) requires you to answer certain questions. Sometimes, the assignment explicitly asks these necessary questions. Often, however, you are expected to decide for yourself what topic to choose and approach to take. Ask yourself these ten questions as you plan your approach:[1]

1. **Formal Conditions:** What are the requirements of length, due date, documentation, and so on?
2. **Latitude:** How much freedom do I have to modify the terms of the assignment and to choose my own way of answering these questions?

3. **Subject:** What, precisely, am I to write about?
4. **Purpose:** Why am I writing about this subject?
5. **Viewpoint:** What should be my stance as author?
6. **The Givens:** What information, assumptions, and materials do the reader and I begin with in common?
7. **Definitions:** Are there key words or concepts I must define?
8. **Organization:** What information, materials, ideas, subtopics, questions, and answers must stand out in my essay?
9. **Beginning and Ending:** Is there a particular point that I must start from and/or arrive at?
10. **Sources:** Which sources can (and should) I use?

When in doubt, ask your instructor before you start to write, but do not ask him or her to answer the questions that appear on this list. Instead, because you have thought about the problem, you can ask for help in deciding which of your alternative answers to the questions would most likely lead to a good paper. That way, you will be more likely to receive helpful answers than if you simply ask, *"What are we supposed to do?"*

STRUCTURE OF A RESEARCH PAPER

The structure of a research paper can be broken down into the following three categories (see Figure 10.1):

- Introduction
- Body
- Conclusion

INTRODUCTION

The introduction provides your essay with direction and interest. The reader will want to know where he or she is going and what to expect. The introduction can provide preliminary information or background observations about the subject under discussion. It sets the tone for the paper. Generally, it should accomplish these four functions:

1. Announce the subject.
2. Interest the reader (by using apt illustrations, factors, or examples, or by explaining the significance of the subject).
3. State the thesis clearly and concisely.
4. Give a route map to the reader, mentioning the main topics or issues to be addressed.

FIGURE 10.1   Structure of an Essay

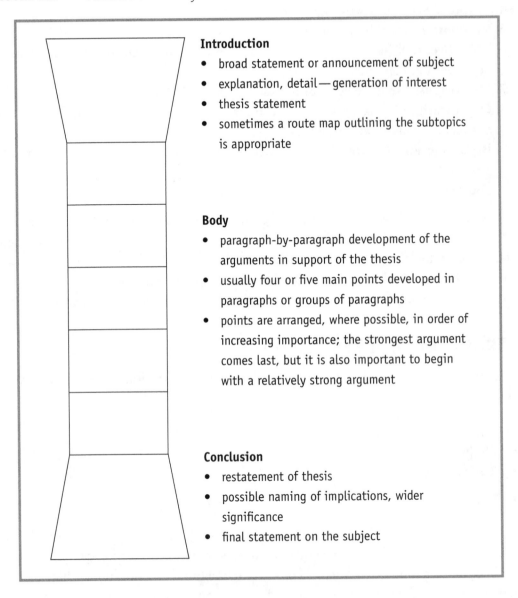

Introduction
- broad statement or announcement of subject
- explanation, detail—generation of interest
- thesis statement
- sometimes a route map outlining the subtopics is appropriate

Body
- paragraph-by-paragraph development of the arguments in support of the thesis
- usually four or five main points developed in paragraphs or groups of paragraphs
- points are arranged, where possible, in order of increasing importance; the strongest argument comes last, but it is also important to begin with a relatively strong argument

Conclusion
- restatement of thesis
- possible naming of implications, wider significance
- final statement on the subject

Body

The body of your research paper should consist of paragraphs that develop the argument presented in the introduction. The first sentence of each paragraph should both introduce the paragraph and relate it to the other paragraphs in the essay. The transition sentences that join the paragraphs have three purposes:

1. To connect a paragraph with a previous one.
2. To point to the content of the new paragraph.
3. To help to illustrate the thesis.

The evidence you present in the body of the research paper should be arranged, where possible, in order of increasing importance with the strongest argument last. As a Good Strategy User, you should also make sure that you begin with a convincing point that will interest the reader in your paper.

CONCLUSION

Several ways of ending an essay convey a sense of finality:

- Summary of ideas with suggestions for further study.
- Personal evaluation of the presented idea.
- Appropriate quotation and comment about its significance.
- Extension of thesis into larger truth or universal consideration.

Naturally, you will not use all of the above methods in a single conclusion. Choose the method that seems most appropriate to the subject of your paper. The basic principle is to restate the thesis and the strongest evidence, and then end the paper without introducing new material.

STAGES OF COMPOSITION

As a Good Strategy User, you can plan the process of writing your paper by following six stages. Set up a timetable that outlines the general planning for the six stages to give you a more realistic idea of when to start the essay and when to move from one stage to the next. Count backward from the date when you want to have the essay completed, keeping in mind how long each of the stages will take. The six stages are:

1. Choosing and Narrowing a Topic or Interpreting the Question.
2. Gathering Information and Creating Ideas.
3. Formulating a Point of View and Planning an Outline in Point Form.
4. Writing a Draft.
6. Editing the Draft.
7. Polishing the Final Product.

CHOOSING AND NARROWING A TOPIC OR INTERPRETING THE QUESTION

If you have been given (or have chosen) a broad topic, you will need to narrow the scope so that your paper has a distinct focus. This will help you to avoid gathering masses of information that you cannot pull together into a coherent package. As you think about a topic, it is likely that you will begin with a broad global theme, but your goal at this stage is to narrow your focus gradually to a manageable scale. For example, the following three titles evolve from a general global theme in sociology to a much more specific topic that is at a neighbourhood level:

- Rural to urban migration
- The impact on city schools of immigration from rural areas
- Social interaction in Pinewood High between the new and old residents of the school district

Gathering Information and Creating Ideas

This is the stage at which you check out different sources to find out what is available. Depending on the nature of your paper, you may find yourself collecting original materials such as interviews with local personalities, browsing the many different materials to be found in your academic or community libraries, or using the resources accessible through your computer. If you are unsure about the best resource, a reference librarian can show you how to find those materials most relevant to your topic. You will not have time to read everything, so you will have to make decisions about the most pertinent sources. Consider checking for:

- ☑ A combination of both old and new sources.
- ☑ A minimum number of sources (six to eight might be acceptable).
- ☑ Specific viewpoints you may have explored in lectures or discussions.

Some texts will require very thorough reading and some writing styles may take more effort than others, so be prepared to put considerable time into your research. Survey a variety of sources to cut down on the time needed to research your topic. Skimming through paragraphs and making brief summaries, for example, will help you to focus on the information that illustrates and supports your thesis. If you input your summaries directly to your computer at this stage, you will save time later during the writing stage. As you read, it is a good idea to make notes on information useful to your topic, such as interesting quotations. Some of the reading strategies in Chapter 5, "Learning from Textbooks," will help you to gather information efficiently.

Read with a questioning approach to evaluate whether the new information is plausible. Do not expect to find any simple answer to a complex topic. Even at this early stage, writing is very important. Take time out from your reading to formulate ideas on paper or computer. Writing and thinking are regarded by many instructors to be synonymous terms. Once you start to write your argument and to illustrate your points with pertinent evidence and references, you will generate additional ideas, and may even change your mind about your point of view.

A word of caution: It is common for students to spend too long in this information-gathering stage before making any decisions. Try to formulate a tentative, working thesis to guide your selection of appropriate information and get writing as soon as possible.

Recording Research Information on Your Computer

A computer is an essential tool for storing and recording information that you find for your paper. Students have many different systems for this record keeping, ranging from writing individual file cards to using one of the custom software programs. Above all, try to create some flexibility in the system that you use so that you can cross-reference sources, quotations, and personal comments.

☑ Create a bibliography by recording (in proper bibliographic form) each book or article that you use in your research. These references will then be readily available to you any time. Adding the library call number for each item will ensure easy access.

☑ Create a file or several files for summaries of important ideas that you extract from the sources you read, as well as for interesting quotations that you want to retain. Although you may want to include in your paper some direct quotations from your readings, be careful to limit the number of these, as your research paper can get overwhelmed by direct quotations and it will lose your voice on the topic. When referencing most of the source material, you will want to paraphrase the ideas into your own words as you integrate them into your paper.

☑ Create a file to record your own insights and thoughts about the argument you want to develop. This will provide you with a rich resource of materials from which to begin writing. The quality of your paper depends greatly on your own insights and observations of the source materials you reference.

A Note on Plagiarism

Plagiarism occurs when students use ideas or words in a research paper without being able to indicate where they found them. If you fail to establish a proper system for storing sources accurately you may not be able to remember the information that would provide a correct reference. In this case, plagiarism results as much from poor record keeping as from deliberate misrepresentation. Take care to identify your sources, to document them clearly, and to think about how you record the material that you want to include in your paper so that you can distinguish between your ideas and words and those of other sources. If you are using information from the Internet, it may be even more difficult for you to identify the author of any specific idea or piece of information. Yet it is very important to reference everything you use since the negative consequences of plagiarism are extremely serious.

Formulating a Point of View and Planning an Outline in Point Form

The Good Strategy User will make a conscious decision about when to begin writing an outline even though the ideas and structure are not fully formed. Try to avoid the trap of thinking that you have to check out all possible books and articles before you start to write down your rough draft. Do not underestimate how your ideas may change and new ones crop up once you start the process of assembling and writing out your thoughts. This phenomenon has been described as "thinking through writing." It may be helpful to refer to the "Structure of a Research Paper" section on pp. 163 to 165 as you proceed to this phase.

Once you have your outline on the computer, you can move ideas around without recopying them and you will be able to check the flow of ideas and logic fairly quickly. However, as only one screen can be viewed at a time, the overall structure may be difficult to monitor unless you print out a paper copy. This copy is also insurance against any problems with your computer. Make sure that you have a backup file for each section of your essay, and be careful not to erase your working copy until you are sure that you have finished with it.

Once you have generated an outline in point form, leave it for a day or so before you write a first draft. When you return to it, you will benefit from having had time for your ideas to percolate before committing yourself to a particular point of view.

Writing a Draft

As you write your first draft, you need to keep your thesis in mind while writing the various subsections. Ideas will flow more readily if you shelve your critical self while writing at this stage. You will have a chance to revise your composition and assess how convincing it sounds later, so it is important to keep the flow of ideas moving through each paragraph as you collect your ideas.

Students sometimes report being "blocked" or unable to write at this stage. If this happens to you, go back and reread the notes that you made while researching your sources. Try to focus on the ideas that you want to express and not think too far ahead to the final product. Another idea is to talk into a tape recorder or talk to a friend about your topic so that you have a rough idea of how you want to present the information that you think is important.

Editing the Draft

When you read through your draft, try to look for certain features that will guide the structure of your paper. Referring back to the original question or topic, you could ask:

- Is my central thesis clearly stated?
- Do I answer the question that was posed in an intellectually convincing way?
- Does my argument stop or go off on a tangent?
- Are the main points arranged clearly and in a logical sequence?
- Do all the main points relate clearly to my thesis?
- Have I used all the main points gathered from my reading? If not, why not?
- Do I see any material that is not attached clearly to a main idea?

Try getting help from a neutral reader at this point. It may be hard for you see the forest for the trees because you are now too close to the material. Be open to reconsidering your point of view based on this feedback. Another option, if you have the time, is to leave the essay for a few days at this point and come back to it with some distance so that you can be more objective. Reading aloud to a friend is another way of checking for structure, organization, and clarity, and weeding out irrelevant material or unnecessary jargon. Check for linking words and/or sentences that indicate clearly when you move from one idea to another. These transitions are crucial to the smooth flow of your essay. (See Box 10.1 for examples of transitions.)

Use the editing functions of your computer to move through the draft as you check for the relevance of each sentence and paragraph. You may find it difficult to discard ideas that you have collected so carefully, but if they do not add to your argument delete them or move them to a separate file at this point. You are not usually rewarded for adding points that are not strictly relevant, and it is not good policy to have the reader searching for your train of thought. This is a difficult step for many students, as they "get attached" to phrases they have written. A concise, well-edited paper, though, will win every time over a long and rambling work.

One useful strategy is to create a new version of your essay (after saving the original) that omits points that do not seem relevant. Put it aside for a day or so, and then read it again to consider how each paragraph is helping to present your argument. You can also use this opportunity to check for grammar, structure, clarity, flow, and vocabulary.

BOX 10.1   Examples of Transitions

Furthermore: this leads to
Significantly: it is clear that
Nevertheless: the underlying factors are
Obviously: this allows for the conclusion that
And so: the following now seems obvious
Finally: all the evidence points to

POLISHING THE FINAL PRODUCT

Refer back to the guidelines on formatting provided by your instructor and follow the instructions as given. If no specific instructions on formatting are given, you can be creative about the format and layout of your paper, the font you choose, the spacing of your headings, and the detail on your title page. Take the opportunity to learn how to make full use of your computer to achieve a professional appearance for your paper. You will be able to hand in a much more impressive paper and save time in achieving correct referencing and bibliographical notation. Run a spell check, although your computer will not be able to identify errors that are real words. Looking at a hard copy of your paper can also assist in making sure that your editing is meticulous.

You may be required to use a style for your research paper that conforms to a certain standard such as the MLA (Modern Language Association) or the APA (American Psychological Association). Find out what style your instructor requires and find an example of that format as a model for your references and bibliography. It is also useful to have available a recent journal article that is written in the style you need. There are many manuals and books that cover these styles in detail, and some are listed at the end of this chapter.

ASSESSING YOUR PERFORMANCE

You can improve your ability to write research papers through your own self-assessment, the grade and comments that you receive, and discussion with other students.

SELF-ASSESSMENT

Evaluate how well you planned your time to meet the deadline, the effectiveness of your reading strategies, and whether you were able to spend enough time on the writing and redrafting stages. Make a note of these points so that you can make any necessary changes for your next research paper.

YOUR GRADE

When you get your grade, can you understand how it reflects the quality of your paper? Note both the positive and negative comments you receive, and try to identify any aspects of your paper that need improvement. Did your instructor question your argument or interpretation, and did you provide enough supporting detail? It is important to understand why you earned the grade you were given, and if you have doubts about it make a point of going to talk with your instructor. Try not to get defensive about your paper and the grade it received. Although it can be disappointing to get a lower grade than you anticipated, you can learn a lot from feedback—especially negative feedback—and if you make the necessary changes, you can improve your future performance on papers as well as improving your writing ability in general.

DISCUSSION WITH OTHER STUDENTS

Finally, it can be extremely useful to talk with other students in your course about how they approached this task of writing a research paper. What kind of ideas did they present, and how well did they do? Maybe you can persuade some of them to exchange papers with you so that you may all get valuable insights about the important ideas in the course and about the quality of writing that you need to aim for next time.

MEETING THE CHALLENGE

This chapter acknowledges the fact that writing a research paper can be a challenging experience. However, writing a paper also presents an opportunity for you to develop many of the essential skills that you will need in later years: researching and selecting ideas, developing your own arguments, and expressing them clearly in writing. You will need these critical skills to be able to sort through the extensive volume of information that is available in our modern world.

The chapter identifies the sequence of activities that go into the process of writing essays and papers and recommends that you plan to complete a number of smaller and more manageable steps. In addition, by planning ahead and allotting a reasonable amount of time for each stage, you can control the writing process so that you can stay on topic and achieve your goals. Keep this in mind as you read Chapter 11, since this writing process has much in common with preparing for class presentations and seminars.

SELF-HELP BOOKS ON EFFECTIVE WRITING

There are many excellent books available to help you to develop better writing skills. Having some of them readily at hand so that you can check out any questions can take some of the stress out of writing. The following is a selection that you should consider for your own library:

Buckley, J. (2004). *Fit to print: The Canadian student's guide to essay writing* (6th ed.). Toronto: Thomson Nelson.

Buckley, J. (2003). *A writing reference for Canadians* (1st Cdn. ed.). Toronto: Thomson Nelson.

Choy, P., Goldbart Clark, D., & McCormick, J.R. (1998). *Grammar and usage* (1st Cdn. ed.). Toronto: Thomson Nelson.

Flick, J., & Millward, C. (1999). *Handbook for writers.* Toronto: Thomson Nelson.

Gulston, L. (2004). *Nelson Guide to Report Writing.* (1st Cdn. ed.). Toronto: Thomson Nelson.

Norton, S., & Green, B. (2004). *Bare essentials, Form B* (5th ed.). Toronto: Thomson Nelson.

Norton, S., & Green, B. (2003). *Essay essentials with readings* (3rd ed.). Toronto: Thomson Nelson.

Robertson, H. (2000). *The English essay: Writing about literature.* (2nd ed.). Toronto: Piperhill Publications.

Robertson, H. (2001). *The research essay: A guide to essays and papers.* (5th ed.). Toronto: Piperhill Publications.

w w w WEB ALERT!

Nipissing University
North Bay, Ontario
www.nipissingu.ca/documents.cfm?itemid=6252
Writing Effectively.

University of Toronto
Toronto, Ontario
www.sa.utoronto.ca/handbook.php?cid=11&sid=47
The Basics: Academic Writing—Some General Advice and Academic Honesty.

Purdue University
West Lafayette, Indiana
http://owl.english.purdue.edu/handouts/general/gl_thesis.html
Writing a Thesis Statement. Note that the OWL Online Writing Lab at Purdue University has a wealth of excellent information about many aspects of writing.

CHAPTER ENDNOTE

1. Adapted from materials by Joan McCurdy-Myers, University of Toronto at Mississauga.

Chapter 11

CLASS PRESENTATIONS AND SEMINARS

LEARNING OBJECTIVES

The purpose of this chapter is for you to:

- Explore your attitudes to public speaking.
- Ask the questions necessary to researching your topic.
- Learn how to structure your presentation.
- Learn how to present clearly.
- Explore the options for visual aids.
- Learn how to relax for your presentation.
- Anticipate the challenges of group presentations.

I f you feel nervous about speaking in front of your instructor and classmates, you are not alone; public speaking is many students' number-one fear. It takes practice to stay calm as you give a class presentation or present your seminar topic. However, presentation skills can be learned and practised. As a Good Strategy User, you can evaluate and apply effective strategies for making class presentations and presenting seminars.

This chapter starts by asking you to check your attitudes to speaking to your class. It then outlines strategies for planning and implementing the steps necessary to your successful performance: researching information, structuring ideas, and presenting information to your group. If you have a plan to follow, you can give a quality presentation and feel the satisfaction of making a positive impact on your audience.

YOUR ATTITUDE TO CLASS PRESENTATIONS AND SEMINARS

How do you feel about presenting in class? You may view the experience as an exciting challenge and an opportunity to share your ideas with peers, or you may feel more anxiety than excitement. Do you agree with some typical comments about class presentations and seminars?

Positive comments: Yes   No

1. I enjoy the challenge of public speaking.
2. I find that instructors are usually very helpful to presenters.
3. I know that others in the group are supportive.
4. I'm actually getting excited about presenting.
5. I enjoy telling others about my research.
6. I value the skill of presenting to a group.

Negative comments: Yes   No

1. I am going to be too scared to speak.
2. My biggest problem is knowing what to talk about.
3. I really don't know what to expect.
4. My hands will probably shake.
5. I am scared that I will go blank.
6. I don't think that I will be able to handle questions very well.

The lists above present six positive and six negative statements about presenting to your class. If you have checked off "Yes" to items on both lists then you are a typical student. Most students experience some concerns about presenting seminars while appreciating the learning experience they offer.

If you checked "Yes" to many items on the positive list, then you are starting off in good shape. On the other hand, if you checked off "Yes" to many of the negative items, read this chapter very carefully as it can guide you in your approach to giving class presentations and leading seminars, and it can lessen your anxiety.

If you know that your level of anxiety is very high about presenting in class, go and talk to your instructor about your problem. Many instructors will encourage and support you by offering suggestions they know have helped other students in the past. You may also be referred to a personal or learning skills counsellor who can help you explore your fears and suggest a variety of ways to handle them. Try to feel optimistic that this is one anxiety that you can overcome and, in doing so, you can reap real benefits. Speaking in public is not just a skill used in school: it is a life skill. After you have graduated and moved into the work world, there are likely to be many occasions when you are expected to talk in public, either to a small group of immediate workmates or to a larger group. When this does happen, you will appreciate the training that class presentations and seminars provided for you.

RESEARCHING THE INFORMATION

Because researching a class presentation or seminar topic is much like researching for a paper, it will be useful at this point for you to reread pp. 163 to 170 in Chapter 10, "Writing Research Papers." As a Good Strategy User you will pose key questions at this stage, and then follow up to find the answers to these questions:

- Is the class presentation or seminar to be a review of the literature, a report on original research, a presentation of my personal point of view, or some combination of these three?
- Has a topic been assigned, or is it my responsibility to generate an idea?
- Can I choose a topic of personal interest?
- What are reasonable boundaries for me to set for this topic?
- If I am reporting my own original work (such as experimental results), am I presenting an interim update or a final report?
- How many books, journal articles, or other sources of information do I need to use?

- How can I survey the source information most efficiently?
- What is the best system for recording key information?
- Is there a theme or angle emerging in the topic that will be the focus of my presentation?
- Do I expect to use a lot of illustrative material such as diagrams, charts, or pictures?
- Is a class handout expected or mandatory?
- To what extent is it my responsibility to generate discussion among my classmates?
- What role will my instructor play in discussion?

STRUCTURING YOUR PRESENTATION

Although you will structure ideas for your presentation in a similar way to a research paper, there is an important difference. The reader of an essay can always glance back to previous sections if there is a problem with the flow of ideas, but your audience cannot do that. Therefore, you will need to address the audience's need for clarity by providing cues about the sequence of topics. To do this, you need to begin by making clear notes for yourself. They should clearly identify the following:

YOUR OPENING STATEMENTS

At the outset, think of a way to get your audience's attention. You can begin with an anecdote, quotation, or question. Humour—if it is your style and is used appropriately—can help to get your audience on side. For all presentations, you should clearly tell your audience what the subject is and how you will approach it. An outline of the points you will be covering will help your listeners to structure information, identify transitions from one topic to the next, and make predictions about where you are going with the topic. You should clearly specify your goals so that your audience is clear about what they should take from your presentation. You may also need to give some brief background to the main topic, but be careful not to detract from your major focus.

THE BODY

Class presentations and seminars are most commonly organized around a small number of subthemes. For example, you might begin with facts and description, then suggest explanations, give examples, explore any debate or argument about the topic, and finish with the significance of the points you have made together with conclusions.

Clear transitions from one subtheme to the next will allow your listeners to follow your presentation and understand it more easily. This is especially true if you provided a clear and concise overview at the outset. Because time can be very tight for presentations, prioritize your subtopics so that you can skip the least important if you find that you are running out of time. Make sure to save enough time for your most important observations.

YOUR CLOSING STATEMENTS

The end of your presentation should be well planned. It may be useful to review with your audience your original goals, and evaluate what you have achieved. If you have to persuade your audience to a particular point of view, then sum up with your strongest arguments—and don't give your audience ammunition by providing the counterarguments at this point. However, anticipate any counterarguments, and have your responses rehearsed.

For a class presentation you will need to have a short list of questions ready that you can throw out to the group if participation seems slow. For a seminar, you will need a much more comprehensive list of questions to try to get the discussion rolling. While your instructor may pick up some responsibility for a good discussion, it is likely that you will be expected to take charge if possible. This is especially true as you move into more advanced courses.

PRESENTING TO THE CLASS

If any oral presentation is to go well, it is important that you plan and practise your delivery. Think of it as a performance, with you as the star. Class presentations and seminars have much in common, although the setting will affect some elements in your presentation. A class presentation may take place in a much larger setting than a seminar, and to many more people, but this is not always the case. On the other hand, student seminars, by their nature, are discussions among smaller groups of students under the guidance of an instructor. As you plan strategies for an excellent delivery, think about the following:

- Rehearsals
- Location Check
- Your Notes
- Visual Aids
- Voice
- Body Language and Appearance
- Handling Questions
- Feedback
- Reward

REHEARSALS

Be very clear about how much time you have to present your material before you have to open up the session to class discussion. Keep this time limit in mind and time yourself as you practise aloud your entire presentation. Try not to rush through the material, as your audience will need time to understand the points you are presenting. You may need several runs through before you get the timing right. Note that it is important to respect your audience by not going over your time limit. If your prepared material is too much for your time frame, edit out less important subtopics rather than trying to talk more quickly.

Over-rehearse the first few phrases so that they are fairly automatic and require less conscious thought. This is important as your anxiety may be at its highest as you begin. Visualize yourself presenting the information while feeling cool and relaxed.

LOCATION CHECK

Make sure that you are familiar with the classroom where you will be presenting, and, in particular, any facilities you may use; know where the light switches and electrical outlets are. Check equipment such as the lectern, computer, projector, screen, and tables, and watch out for things that you might trip over.

If the room is large, try out your voice, and talk to the back row. Even smaller seminar rooms may have poor acoustics; so, if you have a choice, decide where you are going to sit so that your voice projects as well as possible. You need to practise breathing naturally while projecting your voice, as you do not want to appear breathless throughout the presentation.

YOUR NOTES

Think about the type of notes you prefer—notepaper or cards? Even if you don't need to use them, you will feel more confident with a good set of notes at hand. However, try to get away from total dependence on notes so that you can periodically look at your audience and make everyone feel more relaxed and receptive to your presentation. Take care not to drop your notes! However, number the pages so you can reorganize them quickly if, for any reason, they get out of order. Make the subheadings stand out in your notes so you can locate topics as quickly as possible. Notes on a lectern are easier to read, and, because your head is positioned higher, you will be more audible.

VISUAL AIDS

There are several choices of visual aids you can use to enhance your presentation:

- Computer Presentation or Overhead Transparencies
- Slides
- DVD/Video/Film
- Handouts

Computer Presentation or Overhead Transparencies

☑ Computer software such as PowerPoint can help you to format effective visuals, or you can produce individual transparencies. In either case, place only a few main ideas on each screen. Six points on one screen or transparency is about right. Most novices tend to overload the audience with masses of detail and lose the key points and relationships. Remember the KISS mnemonic: Keep It Simple, Student!

☑ Use a font that is easy to read. Arial is a preferred font as it is plain and easy to read. Choose the font size carefully so that the text is readable at the farthest point in the classroom. Try 28 to 36 for titles and 24 to 26 for text.

☑ Use colour and/or overlays to simplify complex information.

☑ Always give your audience time to read the information on the screen before continuing with more information or analysis.

☑ If you are using transparencies, number them.

☑ Don't stand in front of the screen.

☑ Use a pointer to pinpoint specific information on the screen. For a large room, consider using a laser pointer.

Slides

☑ Take care in loading your slides. Slides that are loaded sideways or upside down can soon turn off your audience.

☑ Check that the equipment is working properly.

☑ Avoid going back to earlier slides. Have duplicates if necessary.

☑ Do not plunge the room into sudden darkness or snap the lights on without warning. It is very uncomfortable for the audience.

☑ Keep lights on very low if possible, or have a flashlight handy.

DVD/Video/Film

☑ Check that your equipment is working properly.

☑ Check that you are set up at the beginning of the selected segment.

☑ Avoid using long segments that interrupt your presentation. Also, make sure that this illustrative material is really necessary and relevant to your topic.

Handouts

☑ Consider the function of handouts carefully. They can be distracting unless you distribute them at an appropriate time. If the handout is to be used as an integral part of the presentation, the information should be kept short. Longer handouts with more detailed information are better kept until the end of the presentation.

Voice

On the way to giving your presentation, warm up your voice by humming a favourite tune. Try to avoid a dry throat by sipping a glass of water, sucking a lozenge, or lightly biting the front of your tongue before you begin. As you present, everyone must be able to hear you; so, your pace should be slower and more deliberate than you would use in casual conversation. Aim for the back of the room, and look up at the audience. Pause at the end of phrases to give your listeners time to follow your train of thought.

Body Language and Appearance

Try to be as natural as possible. Move around a little and, if you are overly conscious of your hands, hold something like a pen in your fingers. If you use a lectern, you can lightly hold it so that your hands are occupied. Wear something that is appropriate, tidy, and comfortable.

Handling Questions

Questions in a class presentation usually play a very different role than questions in a seminar. With a class presentation, especially in a larger class, it is more likely that there will be limited time for questions before the class moves on to the next presentation. For a seminar, on the other hand, questions and discussion will occupy a much larger portion of the session. For either case, however, there are some common points to consider:

• Prepare your own questions carefully, together with some points to answer each one. Try to anticipate some of the issues that will lead to more discussion and possible questions on those issues.

- When someone asks a question, check that everyone in the room has heard it, and, if necessary, repeat or rephrase the question.
- Think before you answer. It is acceptable to take time to consider your answer, since no one will expect you to respond immediately.
- Keep your answer relatively brief and to the point.
- If appropriate, give credit to the questioner with a comment such as, *"That is a good question."*
- Do not try to answer a question if you do not know the answer. You can say, *"I haven't considered that point yet,"* or *"I am not sure that I have an immediate answer for that."*

FEEDBACK

Ask friends to give you both positive and negative feedback on your class presentation or seminar, so you get a balanced view. This will help you pinpoint those aspects of the content and delivery that you need to work on before your next performance.

REWARD

There is a lot of work and often a lot of nervous energy involved in presenting to your class. When it is over, reward yourself for a job well done—regardless of your view of your performance. This positive reward will help you to feel better about presenting in the future.

KEEPING CALM WITH VISUAL IMAGERY

Most people feel some level of anxiety before giving a presentation, and you may be no exception. Practise a relaxation technique that can help calm any jitters you might be feeling. Visual imagery can take place in any space—but preferably a quiet place. Sit comfortably, breathe deeply, relax the tension in your arms and legs, close your eyes, and imagine yourself in the pleasant and relaxing environment of your choice.

The two following scenarios illustrate the types of environment that are relaxing to many people. Choose one of them, or use your own choice of scenario, and develop the scene as you continue to relax.

You are on a beach at the edge of a lovely lake with the water just washing over your feet. The water is cool and refreshing and there is a gentle breeze blowing. You can hear the birds calling as they fly low over the water.

You are in a quiet pine forest with the trees stretching majestically upward. There is a faint scent of pine in the air and shafts of sunlight fall between the trees. The path on which you are walking is covered with soft, brown needles.

CONTRIBUTING TO A GROUP PRESENTATION

Class presentations or seminars can be assigned either on an individual basis or to be completed as a group. Group work can be a great learning experience as it is an exercise in sharing responsibility, experience, and knowledge. It often mirrors work situations in which group projects are common. If, as a student, you learn the skills of working as part of an energetic team, you are practising skills that you will be able to apply to many future projects. You need to be strategic to get the group working well as a unit.

CHOOSING GROUP MEMBERS

In some situations your instructor will assign you to a group, but in other situations you may be able to choose the people you work with. If the choice is yours, choose people who are likely to get things done and who show a real interest in the project. It will be necessary for you to meet on a regular basis, so give some thought to how available people will be for those meetings, either in person or through a group chat room online. If you know the other students well, pay particular attention to what they are like to work with, as you do not want personalities to get in the way of progress on the project.

SETTING LOCATIONS AND TIMES FOR MEETINGS

Even if you are using a chat room format for discussing ongoing elements of the work, you will also need to meet in person at critical times of the project. Meet in a location that encourages work and not socializing. You may be able to find an empty classroom or residence meeting room. Generally, neutral space works better than someone's residence room, and common spaces usually have the added advantage of a chalk or white board for displaying information.

Share timetables to find common times to meet and, if possible, choose times that are not open ended—such as late in the evening. You are likely to accomplish more if you have a defined time period in which to complete your work.

ROLES

Someone has to get things started. Always be prepared to be that person if it looks as though the meeting is making a slow start or the situation is drifting. Often roles evolve naturally in a group, but if not then think about assigning different roles to members of the group. If each person takes responsibility for a key task, then the group as a whole is more productive. In addition to a leader or coordinator, you might consider having group members take on such roles as Recorder, Time Manager, Goal Setter, and Summarizer.

THE PLAN

The overall plan needs to be determined as a group. Normally each person in the group takes responsibility for researching, organizing, and presenting one subtheme in the presentation. Go over the assignment together and make sure that you are all clear about the expectations and have a common vision as to what you wish to accomplish, even to the grade you hope to earn. Each member of the group will need to research a subtopic before the final shape of the project is clarified.

A key element to the plan is a set of goals and deadlines. Set up the time of the next meeting with very clear expectations as to what should be accomplished by that time. Make sure that the deadlines are realistic given members' commitments. However, plan to meet regularly so there is an incentive to getting things done.

PROBLEM RESOLUTION

Hopefully, your group will provide a very positive work experience for you. It can happen, however, that groups create frustration for some members, either because of a clash of personalities, lack of a clear plan, or failure to follow through on the agreed-upon plan. You have choices when things are not working out: you can try to ignore the problems and work diligently on your own component; you can air the problems with the group in a diplomatic manner to see if some common resolution can be found; you can see if it is possible to work with another group; you can accept the fact that one group member is not going to be productive and share out some of that person's work among the other members of the group. Nothing is the perfect solution, but remember that group work and getting along with others with different work styles and ethics is part of the real world of work, and your experiences as a student will be a base to work from for later experiences.

PUTTING IT ALL TOGETHER

This chapter has emphasized that an effective class presentation or seminar requires that you apply strategies to research, structuring, and presenting to your audience. You will be more convincing as a presenter when you have spent time ensuring that you have organized the material in a thoughtful way. It is also important for you to consider ways in which to engage your listeners so that they are attentive to the information that you are presenting, and this can be especially challenging if you are just one part of a group effort. It will take time and practice to become proficient in using the strategies discussed in this chapter. However, that time will be a valuable investment, since your ability to communicate your ideas effectively will be advantageous on many future occasions in your career.

Presentation can be an important contributor to a grade in a course. If you work strategically, either individually or as part of a group, you can look forward to some positive results. For more strategies that can lead to success in your course evaluation, continue on to the final two chapters, on preparing for and writing exams.

WEB ALERT!

Mount Royal College
Calgary, Alberta
www.mtroyal.ab.ca/studentlife/study_presentations.shtml
Giving Effective Class Presentations.

Wilfrid Laurier University
Waterloo, Ontario
http://info.wlu.ca/~wwwcouns/TipsForMakingPresentations.shtml
Tips for Making Presentations.

University of Guelph
Guelph, Ontario
www.learningcommons.uoguelph.ca
In the "Quicklinks" box, click on "Fastfacts Handouts." You will find two excellent links, one for "Collaborative Group Work" and the other for "Managing Nervousness During Oral Presentations."

Chapter 12

PREPARING FOR EXAMS

LEARNING OBJECTIVES

The purpose of this chapter is for you to:
- Reflect on the way you prepare for exams now.
- Learn about the three important steps in exam preparation and the strategies that accompany these steps.
- Understand how Bloom's Taxonomy is used to develop exam questions.
- Learn about common exam-review techniques that do not work well.
- Consider how best to prepare for final exams.

In most courses, examinations are a major factor in your overall grade, and so how you go about preparing for them can have a major impact on your success as a student. Exam preparation is easier if you are reviewing course content that you spend time consolidating each week. You will already have a good grasp of the material if you attended all of your classes, have an excellent set of class notes from which to study, and completed all of your text readings and other assignments regularly. At the same time, effective review just before the exam will give you a wider perspective of the course content than it is possible to obtain from your week-to-week work.

This chapter stresses the importance of knowing what to expect on the exam *before* your final review. The main message of this chapter, though, is that your review should involve two distinctly different processes: information gathering and information using. Many students focus only on information gathering—by reading over notes, texts, and other relevant materials. The Good Strategy User, however, also practises information using, through self-testing and active recall of information from long-term memory. If information using is an integral part of your review process, then writing the exam itself is less of a challenge.

SELF-ASSESSMENT OF CURRENT APPROACH TO EXAM PREPARATION

Read over the following statements, and think about how you have prepared for exams in the past. How do these statements match your experience? Score each statement from 1 (this is not typical of me) up to 5 (this is very typical of me).

1. My lecture notes, readings, and assignments are up-to-date before I start reviewing for an exam.
2. I pay careful attention to anything an instructor says about an upcoming exam.
3. I always check that I have correct information about an upcoming exam (such as how much it is worth, topics covered, and format of questions).
4. I plan my review time by setting out what topics are to be reviewed and by what dates.
5. I think carefully about the order of the topics I review.
6. If I am having difficulty with a topic, I make sure I clear it up before starting the rest of my review.
7. When possible I study for exams with other students.

_____ 8. For each upcoming exam I learn the relevant headings from the lectures or textbook.

_____ 9. As part of my review of a topic, I generate my own examples of how to apply it.

_____ 10. I predict and then answer likely exam questions.

_____ 11. I rehearse the whole exam by writing an old exam in exam-like conditions.

_____ 12. I prepare for exams in conceptual courses by reciting the important details from memory.

_____ 13. I prepare for exams in essay courses by writing short essays or essay outlines.

_____ 14. I prepare for problem-solving exams by solving a lot of varied problems.

_____ 15. I make up mnemonics for difficult-to-remember information.

My Total Score _____

EVALUATING YOUR RESPONSES

Each of the above statements is a sound strategy that can help you prepare effectively for exams. As there are 15 statements in this list, each ranked from 1–5, your total score can range anywhere from a low of 15 to a high of 75. If you score at the low end of this range—say, below 30—then you need to work on your strategies for preparing for exams. If you score at the high end—say, above 60—then you have already established a sound approach to exam preparation.

IMPORTANT STEPS IN EXAM PREPARATION

In most courses, exams account for a large percentage of your overall mark. Therefore, it is important that you have a set of strategies you can use in the week or so before the exam that will make your preparation as effective as possible. This section presents a three-step process that includes a number of useful strategies you can use for exam preparation (see Figure 12.1):

- Step 1: Know What to Expect on the Exam
- Step 2: Plan Your Review Activities
- Step 3: Make Your Review an Active Learning Process

FIGURE 12.1   Three Steps in Exam Preparation

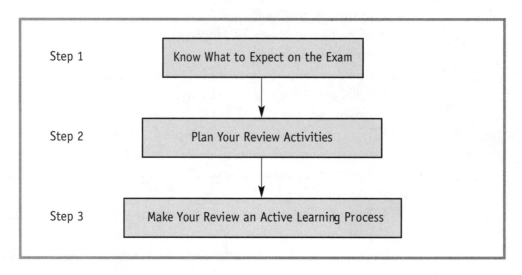

STEP 1: KNOW WHAT TO EXPECT ON THE EXAM

Good Strategy Users find out as much as possible about a test, and so if you already notice many cues about an upcoming test, some of the following may seem like common sense. However, the answers to these questions will guide your preparation activities, so be strategic by applying the following questions to your next test:

- When, where, and how long is the test?
- What format will be used?
- What topics will be covered? Are they from lectures, readings, labs, seminars?
- What special interests of the instructor might influence the topics or format?
- Are any old exams or practice questions available?
- What resources are available for help during the review process—instructors, teaching assistants, other students, Help Centre, the Internet?
- What aids am I allowed to take into the exam—calculator, one-page summary of key formulas, dictionary?
- What percentage of the final grade is this test worth?
- What grade can I realistically aim for?

STEP 2: PLAN YOUR REVIEW ACTIVITIES

Whether or not you are beginning from a good knowledge base, it is very important to plan your review. If you already know the material quite well you can spend much more time practising applying that information to sample questions, whereas if you have a lot of basic make-up work to do you will need to fill in missing information. Here are some strategies to help you plan your review:

- **Set targets.** Choose your own targets on what is to be completed by what date. Setting up a plan with measurable goals to aim for can help your motivation. When setting your targets, keep the next three strategies in mind.
- **Identify topics that need special attention because you find them most difficult.** This task in itself is difficult for some students, and they have to consider seriously which topics these are. You may need to get help during the review process if you are unclear on certain important concepts.
- **Plan the order in which you will go through the content.** This may be tied to the cues that you picked up from the instructor. It is not uncommon for the heaviest weight to be given to the topics most recently completed. Therefore, these should get special attention.
- **Decide where to work.** Avoid settings with obvious distractions or interruptions from friends.
- **If rushed, aim to know the most important topics very well.** If you do not have time to study everything, then it is better to focus on the topics that you want to know really well rather than aim to cover everything inadequately. If possible, target sections that you think will pay off most.
- **Plan ways to evaluate the quality of your review.** How will you test yourself and evaluate your progress? If old exams are available, make sure that you have copies. If there are study-guide questions, plan when you will use them.
- **Make arrangements with other students to study together.** Group study can be effective if there is a clear agenda for such meetings. Plan to do this well ahead of the test.

STEP 3: MAKE YOUR REVIEW AN ACTIVE LEARNING PROCESS

For many students, review means passively "just reading the material over." While this technique is fairly easy to do, it rarely works well. Review **needs to be an active process** that involves you in two important activities:

- Information Gathering
- Information Using

Although your information-gathering phase of the review usually comes first, it may be necessary to switch back and forth a few times between these two activities as your review proceeds.

Information Gathering

Information gathering involves refamiliarizing yourself with all the sources of information for the course. Class notes are often of prime importance because instructors highlight primary concepts in lectures. Other important information will be in your text, lab notes, essays, old exams, and handouts. In fact, test questions can be drawn from any part of a course. This is why the issue of figuring out the role of the lecture and text discussed in Chapter 4, "Learning from Lectures," and Chapter 5, "Learning from Textbooks," is so important. Ideally, by the time you have to review for a test, you will already have summarized your text readings through highlighting or as summary notes, and will not have to reread the original sources.

Learning Strategies for Effective Information Gathering

- **Pull together one set of headings (themes and subthemes).** Often, one lecture topic will overlap with the text topic, so eliminate duplication of review by deciding which source has more "testable" material and working primarily from that. From other sources, add in material that does not overlap with your main source. A good course outline can be the best guide for identifying headings. If you do not have a useful course outline, you will need to generate this list for yourself.

- **Learn this set of headings.** These subthemes are all part of the big picture. Their order in the course is not random, so it is important to try to see the logic behind that order. Recite these main headings to fix them firmly into long-term memory. This should be easier if you see how they form a big picture. Remember that instructors often use headings as a first step to creating test questions.

- **Make sure you have identified, understood, and summarized all the important details that go with each heading.** You can select important details based on the general categories of information, as discussed in Chapter 6, "Effective Memory." For example, key terms are often highlighted as **bold** or *italicized* text or in a glossary. Knowing these important details is essential to successful test performance. You may need to get help from the instructor if there is anything that you do not fully understand.

Information Using

Information using is a crucial and all too often forgotten activity. To do well on a test, it is not enough to be organized and to have read through all the information. You also have to be able to apply the information to answer the test questions. To be able to do this well, you need to *rehearse* the type of thought processes that the test will demand—recalling or applying information to typical test-like questions.

Learning Strategies for Effective Information Using

- **Write or recite all the important details from memory.** When you think you know the information, close your books and test your memory. This strategy is especially important to use in preparing for multiple-choice and short-answer tests that require you to recall the details of information. Although it may not seem so, remembering a lot of new information is not difficult if you can see how each piece of information relates to the big picture.

- **Generate your own new examples.** This helps you learn how to apply a concept to a new situation.

- **Predict and then answer likely test questions.** Because test questions usually ask you to use or apply the important (testable) details that go with a particular heading, you can use the headings to create likely test questions, keeping in mind typical patterns of test questions for that course.

- **Rehearse the whole exam by writing an old exam in test-like conditions.** Don't leave this until the last night before the exam, because errors often indicate topics that need more practice.

- **Spend a lot of time doing varied problems.** If you are being tested through problems, as in science and economics, for example, practise problems that require the application of each of the concepts being tested. It is also very important to review the concepts, close your books, and then do the problems. You need to practise in as realistic a setting as possible where you are drawing only on memory and your own ability to apply the concepts. This is good rehearsal for the exam. Give yourself a reasonable time limit for each question, and if you get stuck go on to the next question.

- **Rehearse by writing short essays.** If you are being tested through essays, practise writing these. Too many students make the mistake of simply reading over material for review, while the main challenge of an essay exam is in being able to write. During your review, get used to recalling from memory and writing in a logical, coherent, and concise manner.

- **Make up mnemonics for difficult-to-remember information.** For example, many students will remember steps in a complicated process by making up a nonsense word that is comprised of the first letter of each step in the process. For more about mnemonics refer to Chapter 6, "Effective Memory."

UNDERSTANDING THE DESIGN OF EXAM QUESTIONS: BLOOM'S TAXONOMY

An understanding of how many exam questions are created will help you to be much more aware of the variety of questions you may expect. One especially useful approach to the design of exam questions is based on the work of a group of psychologists led by Benjamin Bloom, an educational psychologist. They proposed a model—now called "Bloom's Taxonomy"—to summarize typical learning objectives—one set of which was the cognitive learning objectives. There are six levels of cognitive learning objectives in Bloom's model, with each level more demanding than the one previous. This model is commonly used as a guide to writing exam questions, since questions can be devised to test specific cognitive learning objectives. Table 12.1 shows the six levels of cognitive learning objectives in Bloom's Taxonomy.[1]

TABLE 12.1   Bloom's Taxonomy and Types of Exam Questions

LEVEL	OBJECTIVE	EXAMPLE OF TYPE OF EXAM QUESTION
1.	**Knowledge**: Having the ability to recall or recognize specific information that has been learned.	Knowing the definition of a key term
2.	**Comprehension**: Knowing the broader meaning or implications of information.	Identifying the evidence that supports an argument or being able to predict an outcome
3.	**Application**: Using knowledge in a practical way.	Solving a problem or applying a known concept to a new situation
4.	**Analysis**: Carefully examining all of the parts that make up a whole.	Being able to explain or predict an outcome of a complex system.
5.	**Synthesis**: Putting elements together to generate new ideas or a new interpretation after studying an issue.	Linking knowledge from different sources to create or come to a new understanding of a complex idea.
6.	**Evaluation**: Having the background knowledge and skills to make an educated value judgment on an issue, based on specified criteria.	Deciding, based on the data provided, if research conclusions are valid.

Note that "knowledge" recall—often the review goal of many students—is the lowest level that instructors use to generate test questions. All other levels require that you use the information you have gathered, with increasing complexity up to level 6, "evaluation." Many of the more difficult short-answer and multiple-choice questions operate at level 3, "application." Mathematical problems involving the application of a given concept to a new situation are also considered to be level 3. Essay questions commonly require at least level 4, "analysis" of information, and may go beyond to levels 5, "synthesis," and 6, "evaluation."

To illustrate examples of test questions based on Bloom's Taxonomy, here are three multiple-choice questions that represent the first three levels; they are all from an introductory pyschology course:

1. Incubation, when used in the context of creative thinking, refers to the process of:

   a) solving a problem by applying a previously discovered pattern.
   b) looking at a problem from at least three different points of view.
   c) being unable to solve a problem because thinking is fixed on an inappropriate pattern learned in previous problems.
   ➡ d) leaving a problem unsolved only to have the solution suddenly appear a little while later.

This is a level 1 question and, like all level 1 questions, it is straightforward. To answer it correctly, you simply have to know and recall the correct definition of the term "incubation," and then read the alternatives to locate that definition.

2. The "cupboard theory" holds that the mother–infant attachment is based primarily on fear of losing the individual that satisfies the infant's bodily needs. Which of the following observations, if true, would support such a theory?[2]

   a) Even when well cared for, children display intense separation anxiety upon parting from the mother.
   b) Children often display attachments to individuals who have not been caregivers.
   ➡ c) Infant monkeys form the strongest attachments to surrogate mothers that supply food, regardless of the physical characteristics of the surrogate.
   d) There appears to be no reliable difference in the quality of attachment of a human child to mother or father, no matter who is the primary caregiver.

This question, which is at level 2, is more difficult than the previous question. Here you need to comprehend "cupboard theory" by connecting the name or label of the theory with an observation that characterizes its meaning—providing food for the infant. Then you have to read each of the alternatives for the one that most closely represents that connection, in this case *c*.

3. Suppose you lived in a culture in which people were ashamed and confused about eating rather than about sex. Such people might cover their faces and express shock at the sight of another person's lips and perhaps even limit their intake of food to unappetizing pellets consumed behind closed doors. In such a society, which of the following statements would be most likely to be uttered by a person displaying "projection," as defined by Freud?

    a) "As an artist, I am best known for my portrayals of pineapples and Swiss chard."

➡   b) "I always notice Edith's devouring eyes."

    c) "Sure I subscribe to *Gourmet* magazine. Its articles on current events are excellent."

    d) "Yesterday I saw a truly disgusting sight—a huge roast turkey awash with rich brown gravy and cranberry sauce sitting beside a juicy apple pie. I tell you, it just about made me sick."

    e) "I was so angry with Dad last night that I called him a 'baked potato' to his face."

Many students find this question, which is at level 3, "application," to be much more difficult than the two previous questions at lower levels. To answer this question correctly you first need to know that Freud's concept of "projection" is a defence mechanism in which personal negative feelings or behaviours are attributed (or projected) to another person. This knowledge of Freud's concept is then applied to a novel situation in this question—shame and confusion about eating—and the only alternative that attributes blame to another person (poor Edith!) is option *b*.

You can use Bloom's Taxonomy to get a better appreciation of the exam questions you face. Take an exam that has recently been returned to you, and see if you can figure out which level in the taxonomy each individual question represents. You may want to check your judgment of these questions with a fellow student or your instructor. You can also apply this model to create possible exam questions in topics you are currently studying. Choose a topic and see if you can create three separate questions that operate on each level from 1 to 3.[3]

COMMON REVIEW TECHNIQUES TO AVOID

Three quite common but ineffective review techniques that you need to watch for and avoid are:

- The "I Know That" Review
- Memorizing without Understanding
- Memorizing Answers

THE "I KNOW THAT" REVIEW

The "I know that" review[4] is the technique in which the student simply looks at some topic, says "I know that," and then moves to the next topic. The problem here is that *recognizing* information is not the same as *recalling* it and being able to *use* it to answer a test question.

MEMORIZING WITHOUT UNDERSTANDING

Memorizing the definitions of long lists of terms without trying to understand how they fit into the big picture is an ineffective way to memorize course information. Also, Bloom's Taxonomy suggests that to do well on an exam, you need to be able to do more than recall definitions.

MEMORIZING ANSWERS

Memorizing the answers to questions from your study guide, solutions manual, or an old exam is ineffective because it is unlikely your exam will reuse these same questions. Exam-like questions (and answers) from these sources can be useful, but only if used in a strategic manner (i.e., you try the questions as a self-testing activity).

FINAL EXAMS

Final exams present special demands because often you are studying for several courses over a limited time period. You will need to assess the total picture and make some major decisions on when and for how long to study for each course. Try not to fall into the trap of overstudying for your first exam, only to run out of time and energy for the later ones. Much will depend on how your exams are spaced. Answer the following questions:

1. How many exams do you have, and when are they? Mark the dates on the calendar in Table 12.2 to see how they are spaced.
2. To assess your exam activities, record your answers to the following questions on Table 12.3.
   - What course content does each exam cover?
   - What is the format for each exam?
   - What percentage of the final grade is each exam worth?
3. Rank each of your courses in terms of the amount of study time it requires for review:

   1 = a lot   2 = average   3 = a little

TABLE 12.2   Blank Monthly Timetable

March						
S	M	T	W	T	F	S

April						
S	M	T	W	T	F	S

May						
S	M	T	W	T	F	S

TABLE 12.3   Assessment of Exam Activities

Courses	Material Covered	% of Format	Final Grade	Rank

WHAT ARE YOUR SUGGESTIONS FOR EXAM PREPARATION?

If you were asked to help students with their learning skills issues, what strategies would you suggest? In this exercise on exam preparation, suggested strategies for Juan have been provided as a model. Complete the exercise by writing down three learning strategies for each of the problems that Eden, Hope, and Matt have presented to you.

Juan is worried about a major test he has next week. He wants to make the best use of his review time, but not get behind in his other courses. What would you suggest that he needs to consider in his initial planning for his review?

1. Juan should make sure (by checking his course outline, lecture notes for the instructor's comments about the exam, and checking with other

students) that he is very clear about what content the exam will cover and the type of questions he can expect.

2. He should look at the time he has available for review and make a plan that includes what topics he will review, as well as when and how.

3. In addition to re-familiarizing himself with the information (information gathering), Juan should set a high priority in his plan on making his review active (information using).

Eden has just begun her review process for a 15-percent quiz at the end of the week. She is going to start by surveying all of the relevant information. What are three learning strategies she can use for gathering information from her survey?

1. _____

_____

2. _____

_____

3. _____

_____

Hope has already spent time reviewing for her introductory psychology exam tomorrow. She plans to spend about five more hours tonight consolidating her knowledge of the content. Suggest three strategies that Hope can use tonight that will engage her in active review.

1. _____

_____

2. _____

_____

3. _____

_____

Matt knows that his final essay exam in Moral Philosophy will be testing the higher levels of cognitive objectives. Remind Matt of levels 4 to 6 in Bloom's Taxonomy, with some explanation for each level.

1. _____

_____

2. _____

_____

3. _____

_____

ACTIVE, NOT PASSIVE, REVIEW

This chapter has emphasized the importance of using an active review process in your exam preparation as opposed to the passive "just read it over" approach favoured by many students. This active review process begins with an assessment of your current level of preparation of the relevant course material: are you up to date, or is there some new information that you still need to cover? Once you are up to date with your course material, the real work of exam preparation can start. Three important steps are involved: the first step is one of gathering as much information about the exam as you can; in the second step, you plan your review by deciding how long you need to review, what order of topics you will follow, and how much study time each topic will require; the third step gives you a number of active strategies you can use to learn the required course material effectively.

The active strategies presented in this chapter have focused on two crucial aspects of your successful exam preparation: gathering and using information. It is this two-way process that is the key to effective review. If you take a strategic and active approach to exam preparation, you will be able to approach exam writing with confidence. The next chapter, "Writing Exams," presents learning strategies for a variety of exam formats and for managing any anxiety you may be feeling.

WEB ALERT!

University of Saskatchewan
Saskatoon, Saskatchewan
http://students.usask.ca/support/learning/studyskills/abc
The ABC's of Preparing for Final Exams

The University of Cape Town

Cape Town, South Africa

http://web.uct.ac.za/projects/cbe/mcqman/mcqappc.html

Designing and Managing Multiple Choice Questions: Appendix C: MCQs and Bloom's Taxonomy

University of Calgary

Calgary, Alberta

www.ucalgary.ca/counselling/academic/examskillswbk.htm

The Exam Skills Workbook

CHAPTER ENDNOTES

1. Bloom, B. S., Englemart, M. D., Furst, E. J., Hill, W. H., & Krathwohl, D. R. (1956). *Taxonomy of educational objectives: The classification of educational goals. Handbook 1: Cognitive domain.* New York: McKay.
2. Thank you to Dr. Michael Atkinson of The University of Western Ontario for providing questions 2 and 3.
3. For more on Bloom's Taxonomy applied to exam questions, check the Web Alert! section at the end of this chapter
4. Suggested by Marco Iafrate.

Chapter 13

WRITING EXAMS

LEARNING OBJECTIVES

The purpose of this chapter is for you to:
- Learn strategies for multiple-choice exams.
- Learn strategies for essay exams.
- Learn strategies for short-answer exams.
- Learn strategies for problem-solving exams.
- Learn strategies for case-study exams.
- Learn how to manage exam anxiety.

When you have developed effective strategies for your study tasks and exam review, you are ready to learn strategies for exam taking. These exam-taking strategies will enable you to apply your knowledge as effectively as possible and to improve your grades. Success in exam writing is largely the result of applying excellent exam-writing strategies and, at the same time, managing exam anxiety.

There are a number of formats for exams: multiple-choice, essay, short-answer, problem-solving, case-study, true/false, matching-pairs, and fill-in-the-blanks. Each type presents unique demands that require you to apply matching strategies. In this chapter, you will examine strategies for the five most commonly used formats:

- Multiple-Choice Exams
- Essay Exams
- Short-Answer Exams
- Problem-Solving Exams
- Case-Study Exams

MULTIPLE-CHOICE EXAMS

One of the advantages of the multiple-choice format is that the questions can prompt your memory because the correct answer is always one of the alternative responses presented. You may have had this positive experience. However, you may also have found yourself in a situation where you found it impossible to choose between at least two seemingly correct answers, and if so, you share a fairly common experience with many other students. By taking a strategic and step-by-step approach to understanding and answering multiple-choice questions, you will be more likely to make the right choice between those two similar options.

SUCCESS WITH MULTIPLE-CHOICE EXAMS

If you are well prepared going into a multiple-choice exam (see Chapter 12, "Preparing for Exams," for strategies and sample multiple-choice questions), take a strategic approach to processing each question, and keep your anxiety reasonably under control, you have what it takes to do well on a multiple-choice exam. Some of the key success strategies to remember are as follows:

- **Think positively.** You do know the information, and the right answer is on the exam paper. All you need to do is match the two.

- **Take some deep breaths before you begin the exam.** Try to feel calm throughout your body. Let your muscles loosen and your body feel relaxed. Now you are ready to begin.
- **Plan your time.** Although there is a lot of work for you to do in the exam, there is also enough time to do it. However, an eye to the clock will help you to pace yourself. Try to maintain an unhurried but steady pace throughout.
- **Have a system for tackling questions.** If you have a solid approach to apply to questions, you will make fewer mistakes. A step-by-step approach to writing multiple-choice exams follows.
- **Read carefully.** Precision is the key for multiple-choice questions.
- **Be an active thinker.** Do not depend on the alternatives to jog your memory and give you ideas about what it is you are looking for. Think, think, think!
- **Learn from your mistakes.** Look over returned tests and exams, with your instructor if possible, to evaluate any errors you made. If you are still interested in improving your test performance, make an appointment with a learning skills counsellor.

A STEP-BY-STEP APPROACH TO WRITING MULTIPLE-CHOICE EXAMS

The following step-by-step approach to writing multiple-choice exams may help you to minimize errors and improve your performance. The steps include:

1. Cover Up the Alternatives
2. Read the Stem of the Question
3. Process the Stem of the Question
4. Predict a Possible Answer
5. Check the Format of the Question
6. Process Each of the Alternatives
7. Identify the Correct Response
8. Reread the Stem of the Question
8. Eliminate Wrong Answers
10. Guess

Cover Up the Alternatives

It is easy to fall into the trap of reading the entire question too quickly (i.e., the stem or initial statement and all of the alternatives or possible answers). Covering up the alternatives with a ruler or small blank index card as you read the question stem will ensure careful and thorough reading and allow you time to consider what the stem of the question is asking.

If you do not take this first step with care, you may find yourself in difficulty: first, you may skim over the stem of the question so quickly that you misread it; second, you may be overwhelmed by the sheer quantity of information in the entire question and begin to panic; third, many of the alternatives may be incorrect statements and may interfere with your knowledge base, leading to confused recall.

Read the Stem of the Question

Now, read the stem of the question or initial statement quickly but carefully to get a general idea of what it is asking. If the stem is very short, you may be able to arrive at a complete understanding with this initial reading. However, if it is a longer question, you will need to process the question further to understand fully what it is asking.

Process the Stem of the Question

This is where many of the in-exam errors originate. You need to take care in decoding the stem of the multiple-choice question. Ask yourself, "What is this question really asking?" as you try to arrive at a precise and accurate understanding.

- ☑ Underline or circle key content words.
- ☑ Track for limiting terms such as "always," "only," and "never." These words give the statement a specific or extreme meaning that may lessen the chance that it is the accurate response.
- ☑ Rephrase (translate) the question into your own words.
- ☑ Activate your knowledge base and try to remember any relevant information about that particular topic or question.

Predict a Possible Answer

You may be able to predict the answer to the question without reading any of the alternatives, especially if the stem of the question is a complete question in itself and you have recalled appropriate information from your long-term memory. Even if the stem of the question is incomplete without the alternatives, ask yourself the question, *"What do I remember about this concept?"* If you can locate in your long-term memory the original material on which the question is based, you can trigger recall of associated details to help you choose the correct alternative.

This step of predicting a possible answer can be another major stumbling block in answering multiple-choice questions. You may not make the best use of the knowledge you have, because you tend to believe that the correct answer will "hit you in the eye" as you look at the alternatives. This is not so; you need to work on your recall of the relevant information.

Check the Format of the Question

Some questions have combination answers such as "(a) and (d)," "all of the above," or "none of the above." Before you evaluate the alternatives in depth, you need to know if combination answers are an option and, therefore, if you can respond positively to more than one of the alternatives.

Process Each of the Alternatives

Read each of the alternatives for meaning, not just to recognize familiar terms or phrases. Essentially, each alternative is a true/false statement, and, keeping the stem of the question clearly in mind, you need to make a response to each alternative:

- Yes, I think this is true.
- No, I think this is false.
- I'm not sure at this time.

A note of caution: Although multiple-choice exams vary from instructor to instructor, there are three common pitfalls for unwary students:

1. **Familiar phrases from the course.** If you recognize rather than think through an answer, you may get caught out by a statement that you learned as part of the course but that does not answer the question that is being asked. That is, it is a true statement in itself but not a correct answer for the question.
2. **A fact from your general knowledge.** Instructors know some of the beliefs and facts that are likely to be part of your general knowledge, and they may include one of these statements as one of the alternatives as a distraction.
3. **Jargon.** Sophisticated terms can be tempting. You may see a word or phrase in the question and think that because it sounds impressive, it must be correct. In some cases, instructors make up such terms and insert them in multiple-choice questions.

Identify the Correct Response

If you have a good memory and understanding of course content and have processed the stem of the question and the alternatives fully and accurately, then the next step is to circle the correct response. If you are able to complete this step, you have completed the question. However, life is not always so simple, and you may need to reprocess the question using the following backup strategies.

Reread the Stem of the Question

If you were unable to identify the correct answer, the stem of the question may be where your problem lies. Even if it is not, it still makes sense to reread the stem of the question because you will have done a lot of processing since your initial reading.

Eliminate Wrong Answers

If you still cannot make a decision, try to reduce the number of alternatives by eliminating any that seem to be obviously incorrect.

Guess

Guessing is your last resort when all else fails, as long as there is no penalty for incorrect responses. Some marking systems deduct points for incorrect answers to discourage guessing. However, with all the processing you have done so far, you will at least be making an educated guess rather than a stab in the dark.

ANALYSIS OF ERRORS FOR MULTIPLE-CHOICE EXAMS

When you get your exam results back, you can learn much from an error analysis of the questions that you answered incorrectly on the exam. You can look through the exam questions by yourself or choose to discuss them with your instructor or a learning skills counsellor. They can help you check out your main source materials for the exam, such as your lecture notes, text readings, and any study notes you made and used for the exam review. They can also help you to reprocess the stem of each question (i.e., the initial statement or question) and assess how you related it to the various alternatives or possible answers offered. Lastly, they can assess your feelings toward the exam and your ability to deal with stress. Three typical problem areas for students are:

1. Inadequate or inappropriate preparation for the exam
2. Errors made during the exam
3. Test anxiety

As you think about your most recent multiple-choice exam, can you identify with any of these problems? If so, what do you need to do to develop more effective strategies for future multiple-choice exams? For example, if you are concerned about the adequacy of your preparation, reread Chapter 12, "Preparing for Exams." If you made a lot of errors in the exam itself, practise applying the step-by-step approach to multiple-choice questions to minimize errors on future exams. If anxiety is an issue for you, read through and think about the strategies for reducing test anxiety that are presented later in this chapter.

ESSAY EXAMS

Writing an essay within a short time frame (usually less than an hour for each essay question) requires you to demonstrate your knowledge of the course material and your ability to retrieve and organize information to make a convincing argument. The following strategies can ensure that your essays written in exams are well organized and appropriate to the questions being asked.

EFFECTIVE STRATEGIES FOR WRITING ESSAY EXAMS

1. **When you first read through the questions to decide which ones to answer, jot down a few words or phrases for each possible choice.** This will cue you as to how easy or difficult it is for you to recall relevant information for those specific questions.

2. **Review the comments you jotted down.** Use them to guide your final choice.

3. **If possible, begin with a question about which you feel confident.** Budget time to match marks, and spend more time on questions that are worth more. Be careful to answer the correct number of questions. Plan to spend a few minutes at the end of the exam to review and edit your answers.

4. **As you answer each question, plan a point-form answer.** It can consist of the following:
   - A statement of the main or controlling idea that will guide the whole essay (if this is appropriate to the question).
   - Points about content to be considered in order (ideally, one to each paragraph or set of paragraphs).
   - Reference materials or names of important people and events.

5. **Write your essay in a standard format that includes an introduction, body, and conclusion.** (See Chapter 10, "Writing Research Papers.") Remember that someone has to read your work, so keep your handwriting as legible as possible, perhaps by writing on every other line. Also, number your questions clearly in the margin to make clear where the essays begin and end.

6. **As you write, periodically look back at the question to check that you are not straying off topic.** Maintaining focus and logical sequence is important to a successful answer.

7. **Finish on a positive note.** Even if you have doubts about having done justice to the topic, end your essay positively.

8. **Allow some time to check for spelling and legibility.** When you have finished writing, read over your answer and check the grammar. You may be rewarded by the grader if your exam is easy to read.

COMMON PROBLEMS WITH ESSAY EXAMS

Marks are frequently lost in essay exams due to the following problems. Do you identify with any of them?

- **You may not analyze the question carefully enough to decide what key issues are involved.** It is important that you understand and answer the question that is asked. A common error with essay exams is the "knowledge dump," where a student writes down as many facts as possible without focusing on the specific question that is asked.
- **Your essay may lack clear direction.** You need to inform your reader of how the essay will proceed, especially regarding the overall theme. It is important for you to provide the reader with some guiding information in the form of an overview or road map of the proposed order of subthemes. This is easier for you to do if you make an outline before you begin to write.
- **Your essay may lack cohesion because the transitions from one section to the next are unclear or missing.** Pay attention to the integration of ideas and the overall organization and flow.
- **Your vocabulary may be too general.** Make appropriate use of academic language that precisely names the concepts you are discussing. This is a clear indication that you really do know and understand the course material.
- **Your essay may provide an overview of general concepts but lack examples.** You need to include specific examples to illustrate general statements that you make. It is the use of appropriate examples that really confirms your understanding of a concept.

Each of the above problems stems more from lack of thought about how to present information than from lack of knowledge. Do not be influenced by those students who begin to write furiously as soon as the exam begins. Rather, take the time to survey the questions, make a reasoned choice, and plan your answers so that you can allow sufficient time for each question.

COMMON TYPES OF ESSAY QUESTIONS

Three common types of essay questions are:

- Compare-and-Contrast Questions
- Analysis Questions
- Critical-Examination Questions

Compare-and-Contrast Questions

> COMPARE AND CONTRAST the most significant aspects of the role of the Prime Minister of Canada with the role of the President of the United States of America.

You will recognize "compare and contrast" as one of the most widely used phrases in essay-exam questions. It requires you to discuss points of similarity and difference. A common problem is that students tend not to integrate their answers. Instead, for the question above, they first write everything they know about the role of the prime minister, followed by everything they know about the role of the president. However, a Good Strategy User identifies the important aspects of each role on a point-by-point basis throughout the entire essay.

Analysis Questions

> ANALYZE THE SIGNIFICANCE of Canada's natural waterways to settlement patterns across the country. Use specific examples to illustrate any major impacts.

This analysis question calls for something beyond a simple descriptive inventory of waterways on Canada's geographic history. You will need to explore important controls on settlement such as accessibility and barriers, natural routes and their potential hinterlands, resources, trade, and politics. Include detailed examples.

Critical-Examination Questions

> CRITICALLY EXAMINE the contribution of Canada to the United Nations' peacekeeping operations from 1970 to the present day, with specific reference to the cost benefits.

Critical examination in an essay requires hard evidence for points that are made. You will need to provide specific examples, with appropriate costs, in order to reveal both positive as well as negative aspects of Canada's participation in UN assignments.

OTHER COMMON TERMS IN ESSAY QUESTIONS

Besides the terms used in the three common types of essay questions, there is a whole range of terms commonly used in essay exam questions. What is your understanding of the requirements of the following?

assess _____

argue _____

describe _____

define _____

discuss _____

explain _____

evaluate _____

examine _____

illustrate _____

justify _____

predict _____

prove _____

YOUR OWN POINT-FORM ANSWER

Generate a typical essay-exam question. Use one of the commonly used terms from the previous two sections, and state the main or controlling argument that integrates the whole question. List at least six points or subthemes that you would expand on in your answer. Add any references, names, and events essential to a quality answer.

Essay Exam Question

_____

_____

_____

_____

Controlling Argument

_____

_____

_____

_____

Point-Form Outline

_____

_____

_____

_____

_____

_____

Important References/Names/Events

_____

_____

_____

_____

SHORT-ANSWER EXAMS

Some of the points made about writing essay exam questions also hold true for short-answer questions. For example, it is critical that you read the question carefully and answer exactly what is asked. It may be useful to make some quick notes before writing, but, often, because of the scope of the questions, you may be able to organize the answer in your head before beginning to write. This can be a real timesaver.

Before going into the exam, be very clear about the format required for the answer. Some instructors will accept point-form or even diagrammed answers. For example, in your Earth Sciences course, you may be asked to explain the mechanisms that have produced the Rockies, and a well-labelled diagram may be the most appropriate method to use for your explanation. In fact, in some instances, this is exactly what is required. However, in other cases, you will not score high marks unless you present a carefully crafted answer, with careful, precise writing.

Finally, be very careful about making rigid assumptions about how much content is required in an answer. Some students believe, for example, that a short-answer question worth five marks should always consist of five statements. Always base your answer on what you think is a full and accurate response to the question regardless of how many sentences that entails. That is, always base your answer on content and not on a set number of points per mark.

PROBLEM-SOLVING EXAMS

The fourth type of format is the problem-solving exam, in which you must make logical decisions and calculations in subjects such as engineering, mathematics, physics, economics, business, and so on. (See Chapter 7, "Focus on Problem Solving and Labs.") The following strategies are intended to help you avoid common errors that students make when writing problem-solving exams:

- Write Down Important Formulas
- Pace Yourself
- Read Over All of the Problems First
- Start with the Easier Questions
- Write Neatly and One Step at a Time
- Monitor Mistakes That You Are Likely to Make

WRITE DOWN IMPORTANT FORMULAS

You might forget some important formulas in the excitement of starting the test. It is a good idea to record a few of the most basic and important formulas before reading the exam questions. This is a good way of taking some of the load off short-term memory.

PACE YOURSELF

It is important to match time to marks. Many students get hung up on problems that are not worth very much. To avoid this, check the marks distribution at the start of the exam so that you can pace yourself accordingly.

READ OVER ALL OF THE PROBLEMS FIRST

This strategy has two important advantages over just jumping in to solve the first problems on the test. First, you can decide which questions are easier for you, and second, you can do these while letting the difficult questions incubate in your brain. However, use this strategy only if you do not get even more nervous by reading over all the exam questions at once.

START WITH THE EASIER QUESTIONS

Often, one type of problem will be easier for you than another. By reading over the exam (or a few of the initial questions) and then starting with one of these easier problems, you can build your confidence as you write the exam. Also, you are ensuring that you are doing problems that you know how to do before tackling ones that are more challenging.

WRITE NEATLY AND ONE STEP AT A TIME

Many errors happen when work is not recorded systematically. Characters are misread, numbers miscalculated, and important signs are missed. Also, work through the smaller steps in a problem in a logical sequence rather than trying to perform a complex calculation all at once.

MONITOR MISTAKES THAT YOU ARE LIKELY TO MAKE

You may be aware of certain mistakes that you made as you worked with problems throughout the term. If these were of a particular type, watch out for them on the exam. Hopefully, in your preparation, you will have monitored these kinds of problems and found ways to minimize your errors.

CASE-STUDY EXAMS

Case-study exams are most common in business courses, although they may also be found in a number of different disciplines such as nursing and social work. Whether the case studies are to be completed in a short time period (say, 30 minutes) or are very extensive (one case for a four-hour exam, for example), they have several characteristics in common.

- **Make sure that you have a sound understanding and knowledge of the relevant framework.** You have usually been taught a framework or set of categories to consider that you are expected to apply to each case. It may be useful to make a quick notation of the steps to cover in the case before you begin your analysis.
- **Be very clear about the goal of the case.** Where should it lead? It is common to have to make a judgment or recommendation at the conclusion of the case.
- **Set some time goals for the various parts of the case.** Even with four hours for a test, time can pass very quickly. You may have to push on through some of the steps with your eye on the clock if you are to finish the entire case in the allotted time.
- **Remember that reading the case carefully is essential to a good result.** However, you will probably begin to process the case before you have finished reading it over. You may have to do both steps together and highlight key information during your initial reading. Key notes that you add to the margin can be a useful aid when you begin to write your summary. Keep the case framework in mind as you highlight the main ideas.
- **Practise producing calculations before you go into the exam.** If you anticipate that there will be calculations, such as balance sheets, that need to be completed in the case study, review them ahead of time. This will ensure that you can generate the necessary structure in the exam in the minimum amount of time. Case studies usually require a recommendation based on hard facts, and in a business case these will usually be financial considerations.
- **Following the case framework, develop your case summary including all of the categories.** Use subheadings or distinctly separated paragraphs to clearly indicate the various categories. This not only will make the marker's job much easier, but also will demonstrate that you are aware of the case components.
- **Try to ensure that you stay on track and include only relevant information.** All of the points that you make should logically lead up to your conclusion or recommendation. With many case studies, marks are lost because too many digressions are made and unnecessary information given.
- **Pay careful attention to the quality and readability of your answer.** Before you write the actual exam, ask for feedback on your writing skills from your instructor. You can work through a sample case and give the instructor time to evaluate it carefully. You will then know if there are specific aspects of your writing that need improvement before the exam.

EXAM ANXIETY—GOOD OR BAD?

Students experience very different reactions to exams. Some maintain their confidence and control, while others can be overwhelmed with panic and self-doubt. Think about your own attitude. Do you see exams as a threat rather than a personal challenge? Negative feelings and thoughts can be justified if you are unprepared for an exam, but do you experience exam anxiety even when you are well prepared?

Many students report that they feel tense before an exam. For some students, these feelings of tension become magnified into a very real case of exam anxiety. The symptoms that accompany severe exam anxiety—stomach upsets, headaches, rapid heartbeat, or outright panic attacks—can be so debilitating that it can become difficult, or even impossible, to focus on the exam. Negative thoughts can interfere with your concentration. Worries such as, *"If only I had prepared better. This test is going to be so difficult. What if I mess up like last time?"* can make it hard for any student to regain composure and continue with the exam.

CONTROLLING EXAM ANXIETY

Worrying thoughts can be a serious problem during exams. The exam requires you to focus on one particular issue without being distracted by doubts about your performance. As a student, you have to write many exams and, therefore, it is necessary to keep exams in perspective and to try to see them as steps on a ladder to success rather than as stumbling blocks. You need to take a strategic approach to maintaining a positive attitude toward exams. It is best to plan ahead to control anxiety rather than to be surprised by losing concentration during an exam.

STRATEGIES TO CONTROL EXAM ANXIETY

Students find that they can develop more awareness and control of their exam anxiety if they practise certain strategies:

- Several Days Before the Exam
- On the Day of the Exam
- At the Exam Itself

SEVERAL DAYS BEFORE THE EXAM

There are a number of different ways you can rehearse for an exam, as outlined in Chapter 12, "Preparing for Exams." These strategies stress the idea of rehearsing for the exam by working through typical questions using old exams, your own generated exam questions, study-guide questions, and other methods.

Find out where the exam room is, what time the exam begins, and as much as possible about what to expect of the exam setting. Having a visual image of the size and layout of the exam room can help to reduce the number of unknown factors about the exam and can give you a better sense of control.

ON THE DAY OF THE EXAM

Be as well rested as possible. For most students, a good night's sleep is essential to effective performance. Pulling "all-nighters" or studying until the last moment is risky. Get to the exam room in good time, but do not be so early that you have to wait around for a long time. Do not discuss content with other students, or you may begin to panic if you think they know more than you do.

Some students like to bring a lucky charm—a favourite sweater, pack of gum, picture of a best friend, or a talisman. Anything that allows you to feel more secure and confident can help to control exam anxiety.

AT THE EXAM ITSELF

Remember that not all anxiety is negative. Being keyed up or "pumped up" can help you to focus the energy needed to achieve a high level of concentration. You may find that the exam is an exciting challenge—a time to put out that extra effort needed to do well. If you are able to generate positive energy from nervous anxiety, you can achieve peak performance while maintaining a moderate level of exam anxiety (see Figure 13.1). Plan to give yourself a treat after the exam—have a party, meet a friend, watch TV, or rent a movie. This will give you something to look forward to as you write the exam.

Take some deep breaths as you go into the exam room, choose your seat, and read through the instructions on the front cover of the exam. Watch for signs of physical tension. Stretch some muscles if you feel that you are tense. Don't be shy—lots of people stretch legs, arms, and fingers in exams.

Use visual imagery to calm yourself down. Close your eyes and see yourself calmly writing the exam and doing really well.

Focus on positive thoughts rather than negative ones. Inner talk can give you a lot of personal control over anxiety. The following four cognitive strategies can help you control stress. If you can learn to use them when you are not under exam pressure, then it will be much easier to use them successfully when you are in an exam. Don't be afraid to stop and take a break during an exam, especially if you regularly do that when you study.

FIGURE 13.1   Relationship between Anxiety and Performance

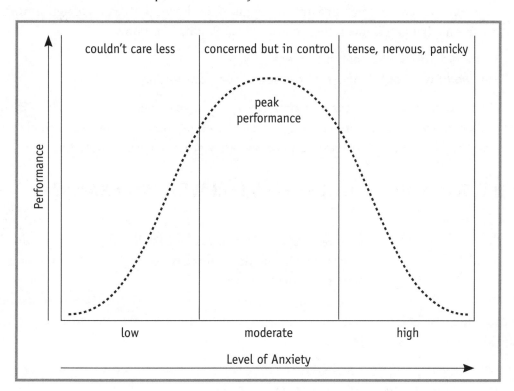

- **Keep your attention on the present:** Avoid thinking of past mistakes or future plans that might involve imagining negative consequences at a later date.

  What's involved here?
  What's the next step?

- **Concentrate on your own approach to answering questions:** Do not get too involved in watching other students in the exam or comparing their effort with your own. You have no control over other students, so it is a waste of time worrying about their performance. Focus on what you know, rather than on what others are doing.

  What do I know about this topic?
  What is this question asking?

- **Keep moving through the questions:** Try not to judge your own effort by criticizing the way you are handling the questions. Stay focused and stay calm.

  Now I will see how I can handle this next question.
  How does the next one look?

- **Control your response to difficult exam items:** Avoid generalizing about the exam experience by entertaining negative thoughts about how poorly you are performing. Focus on what you know rather than on what you do not know.

  What did we learn about this in lectures?
  The world will not fall apart if I get some questions wrong!

If your potential level of exam anxiety is very high, you might wish to check with a counsellor to ask about helpful strategies for controlling anxiety. However, remember that they require time to learn and to practise—they are not a last-minute fix.

WHAT ARE YOUR SUGGESTIONS FOR WRITING EXAMS?

If you were asked to help students with their issues about writing exams, what strategies would you suggest? In this exercise, suggested strategies for Matthew have been provided as a model. Complete the exercise by writing down three strategies for each of the problems that Faria, Pari, and Paula have presented to you.

Matthew turns the first page of the multiple-choice exam and begins to panic because the first question is from the chapter that he did not have time to read. What can Matthew do to stay calm?

1. Matthew can make a decision to leave the first question and come back to it when he has completed the other questions.

2. Matthew should check to see if there is any penalty for wrong answers. If there is, he should make a careful decision about whether to answer that question or not.

3. Matthew can use a systematic procedure for reading the stem of that question, identifying key works and trying to search his memory for related concepts and ideas before he reads the alternative answers.

Faria is just about to begin the last essay question, worth 20 percent of the exam. She looks up to check the time and finds that she only has five minutes left. What can Faria do in five minutes?

1. _____

   _____

2. _____

   _____

3. _____

_____

Pari is about to write an essay question on the history of twentieth-century Canada. He knows so much about this topic that he doesn't know where to begin. What should Pari do?

1. _____

_____

2. _____

_____

3. _____

_____

Paula is feeling tired. She studied really late last night for this exam, and she can hardly keep her eyes open. What can Paula do to improve her energy and concentration levels?

1. _____

_____

2. _____

_____

3. _____

_____

TAKING CONTROL OF THE EXAM SITUATION

When writing an exam, you have an opportunity to show how much you know about the course material and to get a good result that rewards you for your hard work and thorough preparation. It is important that your grade reflects your knowledge of the course content and your ability to apply that knowledge to the specific questions. Because exams are a fact of student life, and you will find yourself going through the exam process on a regular basis, having a system that you can follow is one of the "secrets" to successful exam writing.

The strategies that you will apply when answering an exam question need to be matched with the type of question that you face. This chapter looked in considerable depth at strategies for the most common types of exam formats that you will likely encounter: multiple choice, essay, short answer, problem solving, and case study. Strategies were also suggested for another major exam-writing concern for some students—coping with anxiety. Although exam anxiety is not an easy problem to solve for all students, good planning before and during the exam can have a very positive impact on feelings of comfort and competency and, consequently, on the level of anxiety and performance.

The focus throughout this book has been on strategies and on you as the Good Strategy User. By writing a successful exam, you demonstrate your ability to handle the course content. By learning the effective strategies necessary to that positive performance, you are establishing patterns of learning that you can carry into your career long after the classroom is just a distant memory.

WEB ALERT!

Sheridan College
Brampton and Oakville, Ontario
www.sheridanc.on.ca/career/tips/study.htm
Click on links for "Test Writing" and "Test Anxiety."

University of Manitoba
Winnipeg, Manitoba
www.umanitoba.ca/student/resource/learning/images/Essay%20Exams.htm
Writing Essay Exams

The University of Western Ontario
London, Ontario
www.sdc.uwo.ca/learning/paths.html?topics
Click on links for "Writing Multiple-choice Tests" and "Learning from Multiple-choice Exams."

INDEX

Abbreviations, 58–59, 64
Academic arguments, 131–32
Academic program choices, 18–19
Acronyms, 103
Alternatives, in multiple-choice exams, 203, 205
Analysis questions, 209
Anxiety
    exam, 215–19
    handling, 175, 181–82, 203, 216
    See also Stress
APA (American Psychological Association) style,
    170
Attitude, 5, 6, 12
    positive, 112–13, 141, 202–3, 216

Background knowledge, 5, 11, 12
    for literature courses, 135
    for problem-solving courses, 112
    and reading, 74
Beliefs, 5, 6, 12
Bibliography, 167, 170
Bloom, Benjamin, 192
Bloom's Taxonomy, 192–94
Book reviews, 141

Case-study exams, 213–14
Categories
    of information, 96, 97, 98, 99
    for selecting and learning details, 114–15
Class presentations and seminars, 23, 173–84
    body language and appearance, 180
    delivery, 177
    feedback, 181
    group presentation, 182–84
    handling questions, 180–81
    location check, 178
    notes, 178
    personal attitude to, 174–75
    rehearsals, 178
    relaxation techniques for, 181–82
    research for, 175–76
    structure of, 176–77
    visual aids, 179–80
    voice, 180

Closing statements, 177
Commitment, to goals, 150–51
Compare-and-contrast questions, 209
Comprehension
    checking for, 8–9, 53
    memorization without, 195
    of memorized information, 106
    of textbook material, 76–78
Computers
    access to, 21–22
    in class presentations, 179
    for editing, 169
    and learning a second language, 144
    storing and recording information, 138, 167
Concentration, 150–53
Concentration profile, 153–54
Conflict, group, 183
Connections, among ideas, 102, 132
Counter arguments, 132
Course choices, 11, 18–19
Course outline, 23–24, 135, 190
Critical-examination questions, 209
Critical-thinking skills, 138, 139

Decision Steps Strategy, 113, 116–17, 118–20
Definitions, 97, 114, 132
Details
    of general categories, 96, 97
    of information, 190, 191
Distractions, 151–53

Ellis, Albert, 103
Essay exams, 207–10
    common problems, 208
    common terms used in, 209–11
    strategies for, 207
    types of questions, 208–9
Essay questions, 193
    See also Research papers
Eu-stress, 147
Evidence, documentary, 132
Exam anxiety, 215–19
    cognitive strategies for, 216–18
    controlling, 215–16

and peak performance, 216, 217
relaxation techniques, 216
Examples
in association strategies, 101
and comprehension, 115, 191
in essay exams, 208
Exam preparation
active reviewing, 189–91, 199
final exams, 195
knowing what to expect, 188
personal approach, 186–87
review activities, 188–89
steps in, 187–89
techniques to avoid, 194–95
Exam questions
analyzing, 204, 205, 206, 208
design of, 192–94
memorizing answers for, 195
predicting, 191
Exam writing
breaks, 216
case-study exams, 213–14
essay exams, 207–10
multiple-choice exams, 202–6
problem-solving exams, 212–13
short-answer exams, 211–12
time management, 203, 213
See also Exam anxiety
External distractions, 152–53

Feedback, 171, 181
Filing system, 22, 167
First letters, and mnemonics, 103
Flash cards, 143
Formulas, key, 114

Glossary list, 79
Goals
academic, 19–21
commitment to, 150–51
content-oriented, 20
goal-setting principles, 21
long-term, 19
short-term, 20–21
strategy-oriented, 20

Good Strategy User, 5
characteristics of, 4–9
and concentration, 36, 42
day-by-day problem solving, 126–27
memory, 93, 94–106
and note taking, 60–64
and problem-solving courses, 110–22
and reading, 74–82
Grades, discussion of, 170
Grammar, 142, 143, 162
Graphic organizers, 59–60, 79, 99, 138

Healthy lifestyle, 42, 149
Humanities. *See* Social sciences and humanities

"I know that" review, 195
Internal distractions, 151–52
Internet sources, 161, 167

Jargon, 205

"Knowledge dump," 208
"Knowledge" recall, 193

Lab, 122, 124–26
and course material, 122, 124
reports, 23, 125
time management, 124
Learning resources
campus, 8, 18, 24–28, 175
course instructors and teaching assistants, 8, 23–24, 112, 175
for lectures, 53
library, 161
online, 112
working with other students, 8, 11, 22–23, 27, 111–12
Learning strategies
for effective information gathering, 190
for effective information using, 190–91
and personal learning style, 9, 12, 53
purpose of, 4
self-management strategies, 6, 110
thinking strategies, 6, 8–9, 110, 113–22
vs. good intentions, 7–8

Learning style, ix–xiii, 9, 12, 53–54
Lecture notes, 8, 52, 55–57, 60–64
Lecture strategies, 50–68
    active listening, 8, 53, 54–55, 64
    comprehension, 53, 111
    preparation, 52–53, 64
    for problem-solving courses, 111
    reviewing notes, 63–64
    taping, 64, 65
Legibility, 207
Listening skills, 8, 53, 54–55, 64, 143
Literature courses, 132, 134–41
    critical perspectives in, 136–37
    critical-thinking skills, 138, 139
    literary elements, 136
    preparation for, 135
    recording system, 138
Loci mnemonic, 103–4

Main ideas, 77
Meetings, for group presentations, 182
Memorization, without comprehension, 195
Memory
    association strategies, 101–4
    and connection between ideas, 102
    consolidating information, 99–104
    long-term, 94
    mnemonics, 9, 102–4, 191
    repetition and, 143
    review and/or rehearsal strategies, 104–5
    sensory, 92–93
    short-term, 93–94
    structured, 94–99
    and visual imagery, 101–2
Mistakes, learning from, 203, 206, 213
MLA (Modern Language Association) style, 170
Mnemonics, 9, 102–4, 191
Multiple-choice exams, 202–6
Multiple-choice questions, 193–94

Note taking
    highlighting key ideas, 78–79, 80
    lectures, 55–56, 57–59, 60–63
    summary notes, 78, 79, 81, 167

Opening statements, 167

Paraphrasing, 77
Plagiarism, 167
Prediction
    of possible answer, 204
    of possible exam questions, 191
Preparation
    for class, 5, 8, 52, 135
    for lab, 124
    for language course, 142
Problem solving, 110–22, 128
    Concept Summary Strategy, 113–16
    conceptual approach, 111, 113
    Decision Steps Strategy, 113, 116–17, 118–20
    exam preparation, 191
    guidelines for, 110–13
    kinds of difficult problems, 114
    mathematical problems, 193
    practice problems, 110–11, 112
    Range of Problems Strategy, 113, 117, 121–22, 123
    time management in, 111
Problem-solving exams, 212–13
Procrastination
    remedies for, 46
    symptoms of, 43–44
    understanding, 44–45

Questions, role of
    in class presentations and seminars, 180–81
    learning objectives, 192–94
    in reading, 76, 79
    in rehearsal strategies, 105
    See also Exam questions

Range of Problems Strategy, 113, 117, 121–22, 123
Reading ahead, 5, 135
    See also Preparation, for class
Reading strategies, 11, 69–87
    asking questions, 76, 79
    background knowledge, 74
    goal setting, 72–74
    note taking, 78–79
    outlining, 75

reflecting on material, 76–78
scanning, 84–85
skimming, 84
speed, 82
SQ4R system, 74–82
surveying of material, 74
Red herrings, 121
Referencing, 161, 167, 170
Rehearsal strategies, 104–5, 178, 191
Relaxation techniques, 149, 181–82, 216
Research papers, 159–72
analysis in, 160
assignment, 162–63
documentation, 161
draft, 168
editing, 168–69
final product, 170
ideas, thoughts, and insights, 166–67
language and presentation, 162
organization, 162
outline, 168
performance assessment, 170–71
research tools, 161
sources, 161, 166–67
stages of composition, 165–70
structure of, 163–65
style, 162, 170
thesis, 160–61
time management, 167
topic choice, 165–66
Reviewing
as active process, 189–91
for consolidating information, 104–5
lecture notes, 63–64
reading material, 79
Rewards, 181
Rhymes, 103
Roles, in group presentations, 182–83

Secondary sources, 138, 141
Second language courses, 141–44
Self-assessment
academic reading, 70
lectures, 51–52
time management, 32–33
Self-help books, 171

Self-talk, 148
Self-tests, 143
Selye, Hans, 147
Seminars. *See* Class presentations and seminars
Short-answer exams, 211–12
Short-answer questions, 193
Skimming, 166
Sleep, and rest, 149, 216
Social sciences and humanities, disciplines, 131
Sounds, and mnemonics, 103
Spelling, 162, 207
Strategic awareness, 9, 12
common problems, 208
types of questions, 208–9
Stress, 146–56
coping strategies, 148–49
effects of, 147
individual responses to, 147–48
and lifestyle, 149
See also Anxiety
Structured memory
creating, 96–105
storage of information, 95–96
Study environment, 7–8, 21–22, 152–53
Study group, 22–23
Summarizing, 94, 97, 138, 139, 140, 190
Support network, 150

Textbooks, 72
chapter headings, 74, 75, 76–77
and course work, 71–72
layout of, 77
Thesis, 160–61
Thesis statement, 137
Time management, 30–49
analyzing time spent, 39
assessing priorities, 34
common problems, 31
efficient use of time, 36, 42–43
evaluating personal approach to, 32, 33
in exam writing, 203, 213
goals, 20
for healthy lifestyle, 42
for language courses, 142
planning, 4, 35–36
for reading, 73

regular assessment of, 39
scheduling, 8
for solving problems, 111
for studying, 43
system, 33–42
Titles
chapter headings, 74, 75, 76–77
of concepts, 114
for memory structure, 96, 99, 132, 133–34, 190

Transitions
in oral presentations, 176–77
in writing, 169, 208
Visual imagery, 101, 181–82, 216
Vocabulary, 82–83, 142, 208

Working backward, 121, 122